ELECTRIC BASS for guitarists

National Guitar Workshop Book
Approved Curriculum

THE GUITARIST'S GUIDE TO PLAYING THE BASS

D1743074

table of contents

*This book was acquired, edited and produced
by Workshop Arts, Inc., the publishing arm of
the National Guitar Workshop.*
Nathaniel Gunod: acquisitions, managing editor
Joe Bouchard: music typesetter
Timothy Phelps: interior design, photos on page 44
CD performed and recorded by Joe Bouchard

Cover photo: Karen Miller
Cover model: Rich Lackowski
Guitar courtesy of: Schecter Guitar Research

ISBN 0-7390-3335-2 (Book & CD)

Alfred

INTRODUCTION

This book is for you if you already play the guitar, but have decided to learn something about playing the bass. We will be talking about playing the standard, four-string electric bass.

There are several reasons why guitarists end up playing the bass. First is probably necessity:

1. There just aren't that many bass players out there, and often the only way to have a bass player in the band is for one of the guitarists to take the job.

Second is probably career savvy:

2. If you're trying to make a living as a musician, the more diverse you are, the more in-demand you will be. Again, there aren't that many bass players out there, so anyone who's ready, willing and able is sure to find playing opportunities.

Third may be pure interest:

3. Many guitarists occasionally wish they could be the one laying down the groove and knocking out those cool, funky bass lines.

All of these are good enough reasons to go ahead and give it a try. After all, the bass is technically a "bass *guitar*," and stepping over to the bass is not that big a step. It is bigger than many realize, however, which is where this book comes in.

If you have a rock band that needs a bass player, the most important thing is that you understand how the role of the bass player differs from that of a guitarist's, and that you are ready to fill that role. This book will help you understand about laying down a groove and playing with the drummer so that you can help your band sound like a tight, ready-to-rock unit.

This book assumes you play the guitar and know a little bit about chords and guitar music. A brief review of the basics of reading notation and tablature is included in the beginning.

But here is where we find one of the big differences between guitar and bass: Bass players read a different clef. If number 2 in the list above describes you to any degree, this is an important issue for you. Opportunities exist for people that can sit down and sight-read a bass part. It could be anything from sitting in with a theater pit-orchestra to a gig with a stage band to a wedding gig reading from a fake book. This book will help you prepare for these opportunities.

Bass techniques such as slop and pop are introduced and there are plenty of example bass lines included, so if you just want try some bass-player shoes on for size, there's plenty here for you to do.

Have fun!

ACKNOWLEDGEMENTS
Many of the ideas in this book were inspired by the work of Dave Overthrow, an outstanding musician and bass player and the author of *The Complete Electric Bass Method*, also published by Alfred and The National Guitar Workshop. The slap and pop bass lines in the last chapter are from his book, *Intermediate Electric Bass.*

A compact disc is included with this book. This disc can make learning with the book easier and more enjoyable. The symbol shown at the left appears next to every example that is on the CD. Use the CD to help ensure that you're capturing the feel of the examples and interpreting the rhythms correctly. The numeral below the symbol corresponds directly to the CD track number. Track 1 provides tuning notes for your bass.

LESSON 1
The Basics

THE BASS FRETBOARD

As you may have already realized, the four strings of the bass are tuned exactly the same as the bottom four strings of your guitar, from bottom to top: E-A-D-G. And while the guitar is already quite a low-sounding instrument, the bass is a full octave (12 half steps, or 12 frets) lower. The diagram below shows all of the notes on the bass fretboard.

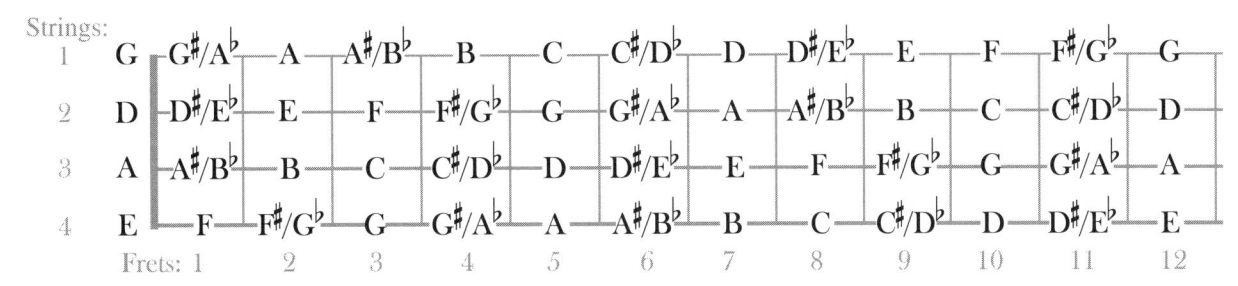

Summary: The bass sounds an octave lower than the guitar and shares the same notes:

Bass 4th string   =   Guitar 6th string (E)
Bass 3rd string   =   Guitar 5th string (A)
Bass 2nd string   =   Guitar 4th string (D)
Bass 1st string   =   Guitar 3rd string (G)

TUNING THE BASS

Tuning the bass is the same as tuning the guitar. Your ears will have to adjust to the lower octave, but you can make the job a little easier by tuning your 12th-fret notes (or even better, the 12th-fret harmonics) to the open strings of a guitar.

Many players will hedge their bets by plugging into an electronic tuner, which will guarantee success. It won't tune the bass for you, but it will tell you when you have each string set to the correct pitch.

Here's the tried and true method for tuning the strings relative to one another.

Step 1. Tune the 12 fret of the 4th string (the lowest-sounding string) to the open 6th string of a tuned guitar; or tune the open 4th string to the low E of a keyboard (19 white keys below middle C).

Step 2. Match the open 3rd string A to the A on the 5th fret of the 4th string.

Step 3. Match the open 2nd string D to the D on the 5th fret of the 3rd string.

Step 4. Match the open 1st string G to the G on the 5th fret of the 2nd string.

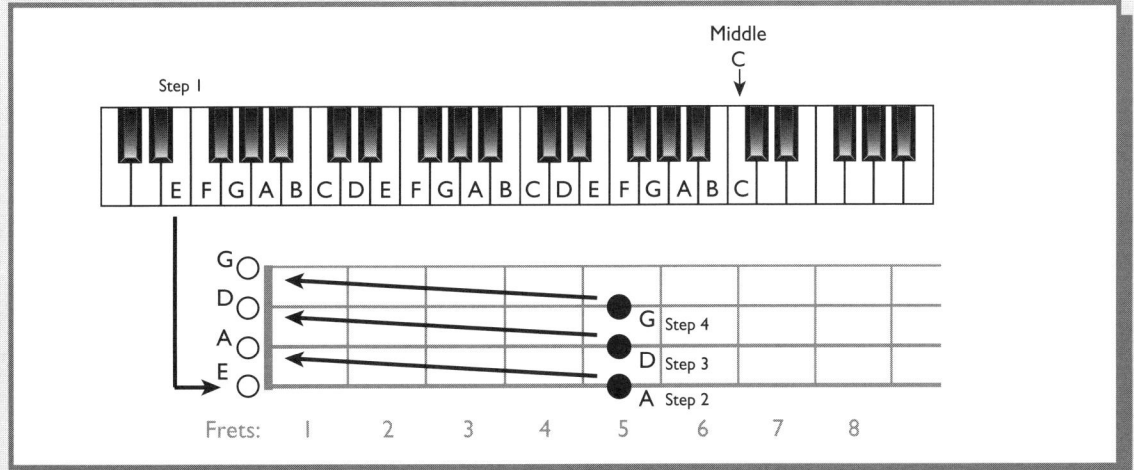

LESSON 2
Plucking the Strings

As you have probably noticed, most bass players use the index and middle fingers of their right hand to pluck the strings (if you are left-handed and reverse your instrument to play, just reverse these instructions). If you are going to be a switch hitter and play both bass and guitar, you may choose to play the bass with a pick. There are no hard-and-fast rules about this, but many bass players prefer the sound of fingers on the strings to the sound of the pick. Soft picks made especially for playing the electric bass are available, and these make a less obvious picking sound. The choice is completely up to you, and usually determined by the kind of music you play and the kind of sound you want to make.

If you are going to learn standard finger-plucking technique, be prepared for a few weeks of discomfort while your right-hand calluses develop and catch up to those on your left hand.

Here are the symbols we will use for plucking the strings. They are the same as those commonly used for picking in guitar music and for bowing in music for acoustic double bass and other members of the violin family.

∏ = Pluck with the index finger or down with the pick.

∨ = Pluck with the middle finger or up with the pick.

Here are some technical guidelines for using the fingers to pluck the strings:

Keep your fingers and wrist as relaxed as possible. Use a rest stroke. A rest stroke is executed by pulling the tip of the finger across the string so that it lands on the next adjacent string.

You can anchor your thumb on the pickup (or even on the 4th string while playing the other three strings) for added stability.

Prepare the finger on the string.

Pull across, landing with the tip of your finger on the next string.

When playing the 4th string, there is no string to land on. You can land against your thumb.

LESSON 3
Reading Music for the Bass

PITCH

Reading music for the bass is the same as for the guitar in that there is a *staff* with five lines and four spaces on which *notes* are placed to tell us which *pitch* (degree of highness or lowness) to play.

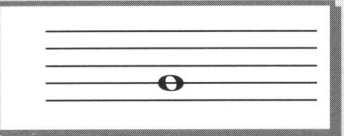

For the notes, we have the same musical alphabet as we do for guitar, A–B–C–D–E–F–G, but the *clef* is different. Guitar music uses a *treble clef*, also called the *G clef* because its tail encircles the G line.

Bass music uses a *bass clef*, also called an *F clef*, because its dots surround the F line.

One helpful trick for learning to read bass clef is to notice that a bass-clef note has the same name as a treble-clef note one line or one space higher. For example, in treble clef, the first line is F. In bass clef, the second line of the staff is F. In treble clef, the first space is E. In bass clef, the second space is E.

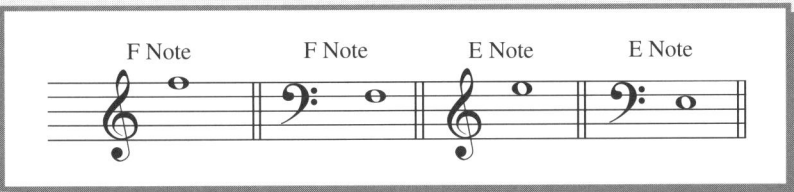

Here is the low E (open 6th string) of your guitar on the staff in treble clef compared to the very same E on the bass (2nd fret, 2nd string) on the staff in bass clef.

Here is an exercise for learning to read music written in the bass clef. Write the names of the notes on the lines under the staff. Since you know that the second line from the top is F, you should be able to figure these out. You can check your answers on the bottom of page 6.

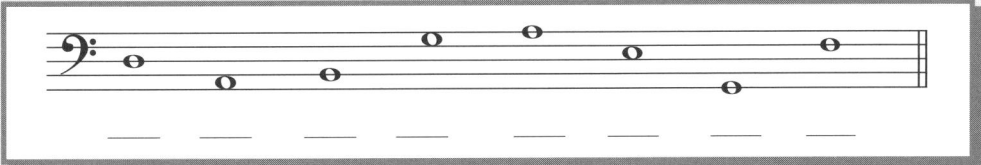

TIME

BEATS AND MEASURES

Measures divide music into groups of *beats.* A beat is a division of time that is the basic pulse behind the music. The vertical lines that cross the staff are called *bar lines* and they show where one measure begins and another ends. *Double bars* mark the end of a section or a short example.

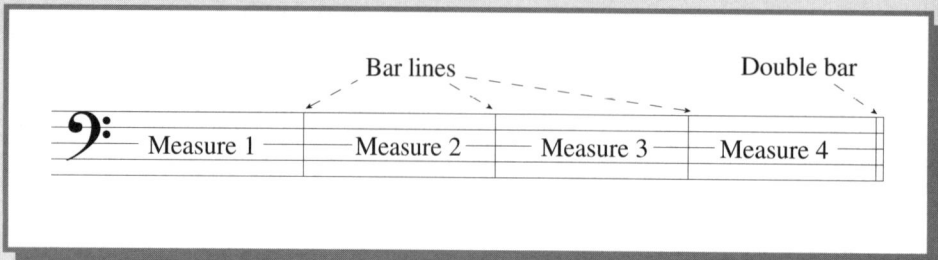

NOTE DURATIONS

As you learned on page 5, the location of a note relative to the staff tells us its pitch (how high or low it is). The *duration*, or *value*, is indicated by its appearance. A whole note is given four beats, a half note two and a quarter note one.

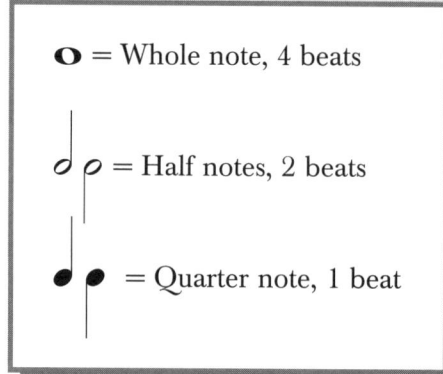

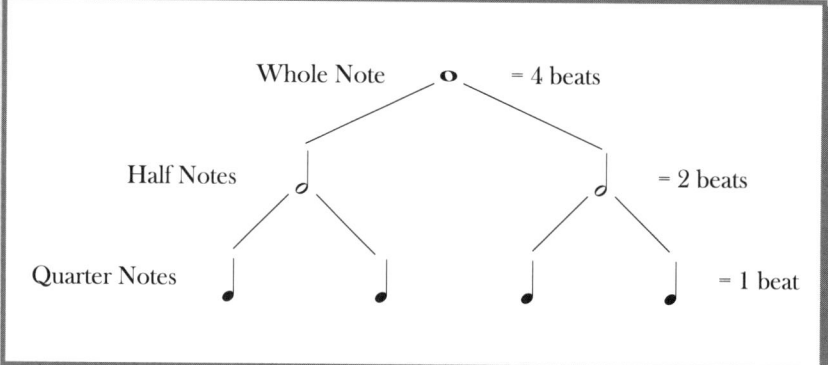

TIME SIGNATURES

At the beginning of any piece or song, you'll find a time signature. A time signature consists of two numbers. The top number tells you how many beats are in each measure. The bottom number tells you what kind of note gets one beat, and is usually a **4**, to represent a quarter note. The most common time signature, often called common time, is $\frac{4}{4}$.

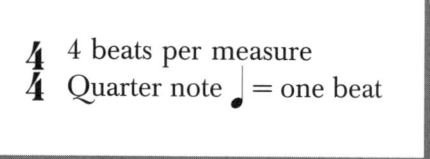

ANSWERS TO QUIZ ON PAGE 5.

LESSON 4
Reading in Open Position

As with the guitar, open position refers to the first few frets and the open strings. The following two pages will get you started reading music for the bass in this position. We will use tablature in some sections of this book, but not in the lessons entitled "reading." These lessons are included to help prepare you for situations where reading is required. In those real-life situations, tablature is not provided.

THE 1ST AND 2ND STRINGS

Here are the notes in open position on the 1st and 2nd strings.

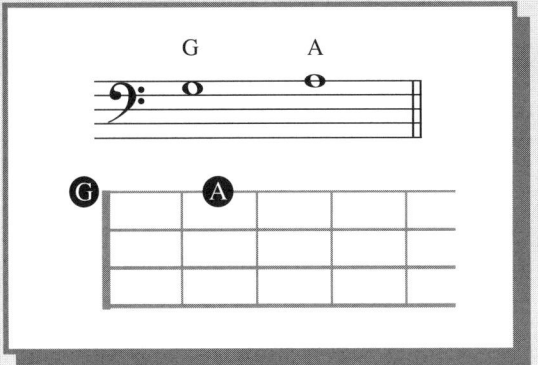
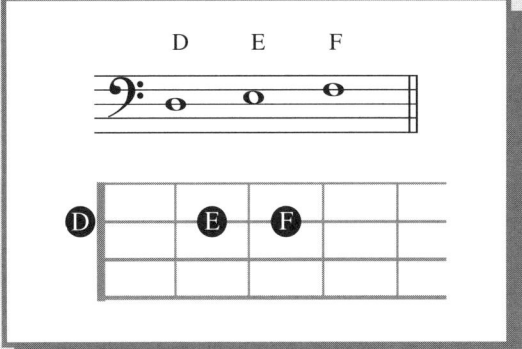

Now practice reading and playing the following exercises. If you are new to reading music, count aloud "1, 2, 3, 4, 1, 2, 3, 4," and so on. Count evenly and slowly, being careful to give each note its correct value. It is a good idea to practice with a metronome, which is an adjustable device that provides a click with which you can play. Set it to a reasonably low number, such as 52 or below (the lower the number, the slower the tempo or speed). Work on playing exactly with the clicks, as you would with a drummer.

In these exercises, use the 2nd finger of your left hand to play notes on the 2nd fret, and the 3rd finger to play notes on the 3rd fret.

THE 3RD AND 4TH STRINGS

Notice that the lowest note on the bass, E on the open 4th string, is written with a ledger (sometimes spelled leger) line. This little line extends the staff downward by one or more lines. Ledger lines are also used to extend the staff upward for some of the higher notes on the bass.

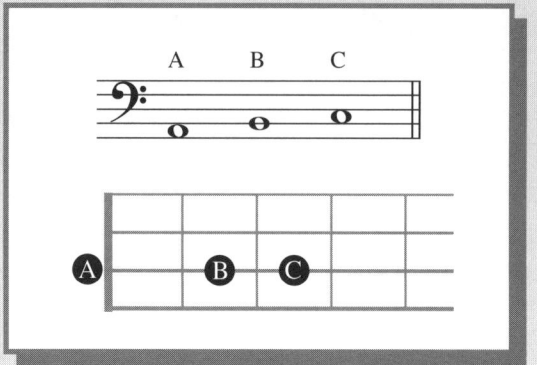 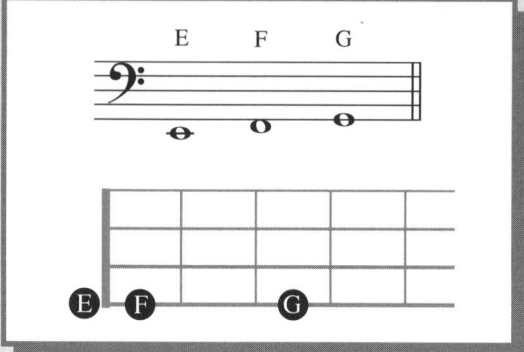

Practice reading and playing these exercises.

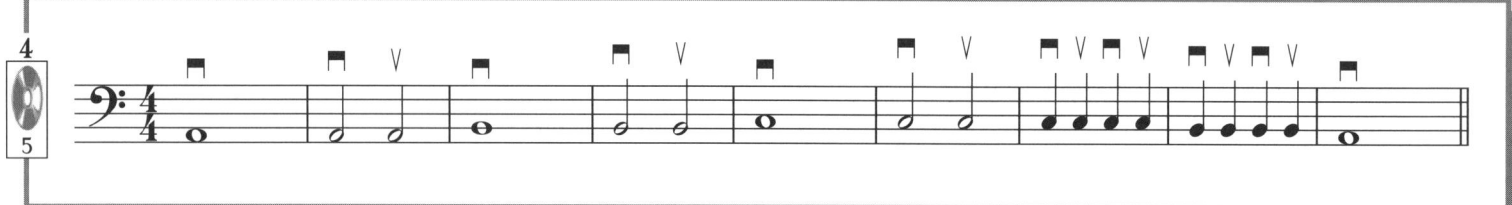

Use your left-hand 1st finger for the low F on the 1st fret of the 4th string.

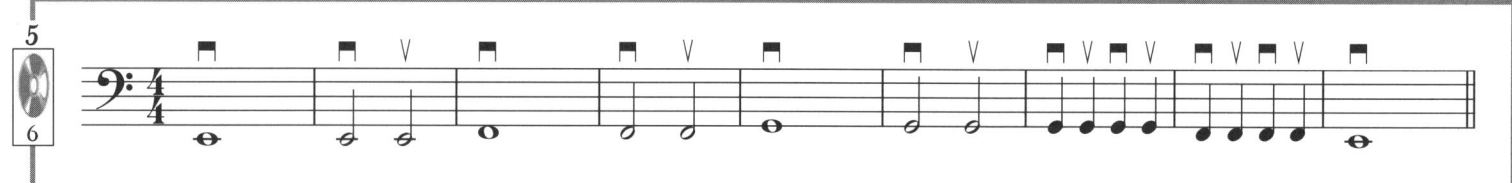

ACCIDENTALS

Accidentals alter notes or return them to their normal positions after being altered.

♯   Sharp. This sign raises a note one half step (one fret).

♭   Flat. This sign lowers a note one half step.

♮   Natural. This sign returns a note that has been sharped or flatted to its original pitch and position.

An accidental only counts for the measure in which it appears, so the natural sign is only used when the natural note is needed in a measure in which it has been altered by a sharp or flat. Try reading these exercises that include accidentals.

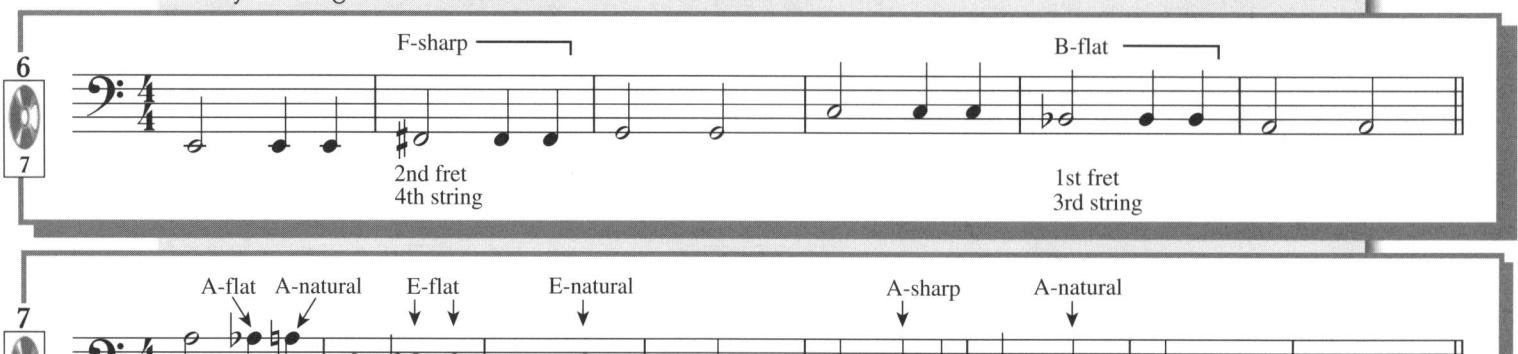

LESSON 5
Playing Bass Lines Along with Chords and Reading Tablature

If you have taken up the bass to fill a spot in your band, the easiest place for you to start is with watching the guitarist's hands. You have played all or most of the chords they'll be playing, so you can easily learn to recognize them. Then, it's a simple matter of playing something that supports those chords.

PLAY THE NOTES IN THE CHORD

As you know, every chord has a letter name, such as C or G. That letter name comes from the root of the chord. For example, the C-note on the 3rd fret of the guitar's 5th string is the root of the C chord. On the bass, that note is on the 3rd string, 3rd fret.

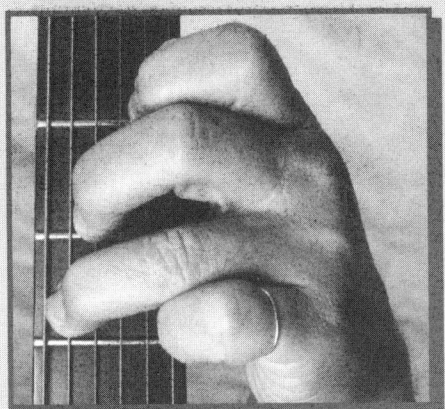
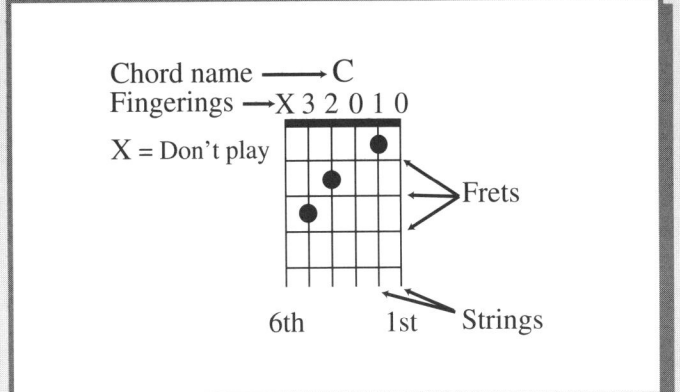

It is important to learn all of the notes in every chord, so that you can use them in a bass line. Notice that some notes occur more than once.

Here are the bass notes for the C chord on the staff.

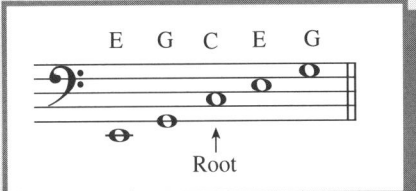

Let's try using the notes of the C chord to play a bass line along with a C chord. Listen to the bass player play with the band on the CD, and then use your balance control on your stereo to dial him out and step in and play with the band.

If this is your first time reading tablature (TAB), relax; it's easy. The lowest line is the lowest (4th) string. The numbers represent the frets. You'll still need to refer to the standard music notation for the rhythms. The numbers below the TAB tell you which left-hand fingers to use.

THE ROLE OF THE BASS PLAYER: PART 1– REINFORCE THE HARMONY

Take another look at example 8 on page 9 and notice the pitch that is played most often is the root of the C chord (C). One of your most important functions as a bass player is to support the harmony (chords). It is the singer's (or lead instrument's) job to play the melody, the guitarist's and/or keyboard player's job(s) to play the harmony and the drummer's job to play the rhythm. You are so important that you have two main jobs: support the harmony and support the rhythm. We'll talk more about supporting what the drummer is doing later. For now, make sure you are always reinforcing the harmony with the root. The downbeat (the first beat of a measure) is the strongest beat, and the most important place for the root to be played.

MAJOR CHORD SHAPES

It is going to be very useful for you to have a memorized library of major-chord patterns from which to choose notes to play. These patterns will be most useful if they are easily *transposable* to any root. To *transpose* means to change the pitch level. A pattern with no open strings is the easiest kind to transpose. We simply move the pattern to the appropriate root when the chord changes.

Following are two easily transposable patterns for playing with major chords. Notice that they include two new notes: the G on the 5th fret of the 2nd string (substitutes for the open string, in fact you use this G to tune the 1st string G), and the high C on the 5th fret of the 1st string. It is most helpful to think of the patterns, which is why the neck diagram illustrations are shown. Play up and down through these patterns until they are second nature to you.

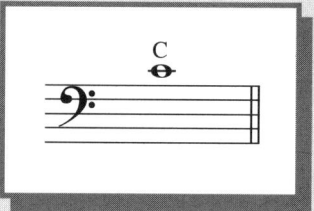

ROOT ON THE 3RD STRING

The first pattern is for playing low roots on the 3rd string. Notice that it calls for the 2nd finger on the low root, and the 4th finger (or pinky) on the high G and new high C. You may be quite accustomed to using the 4th finger in your guitar playing. If not, just take it slow and give it time to coordinate with the other fingers.

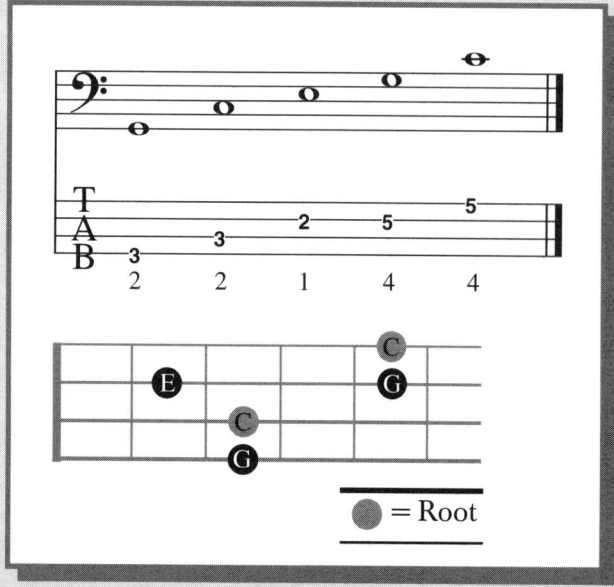

ROOT ON THE 4TH STRING

This pattern is exactly the same as the first except the low root is now on the 4th string.

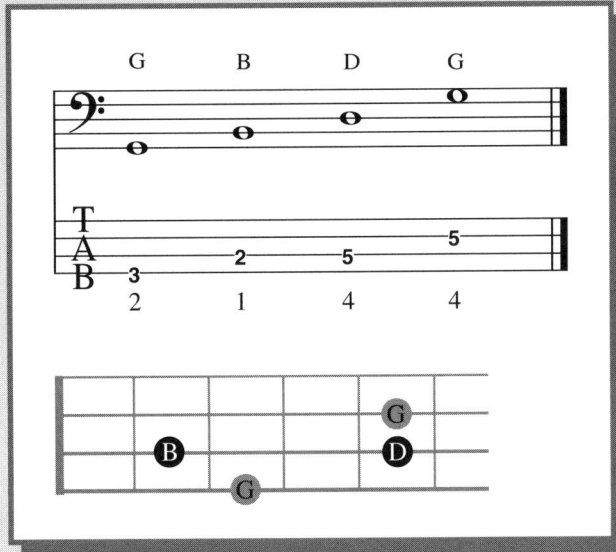

This is a typical chord progression (series of chords) in the key of G. The patterns being used are labeled and the basic guitar chord shapes are shown above the music. Notice that there is one new note: high D.

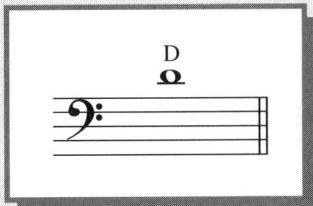

After listening to the CD, practicing by yourself and then with the CD, have a friend strum a steady rhythm, randomly changing between these chords on each downbeat. Try to become fluent at identifying the chord your friend is playing and changing between the two patterns. Notice that every note in the bass line belongs to the chord being played.

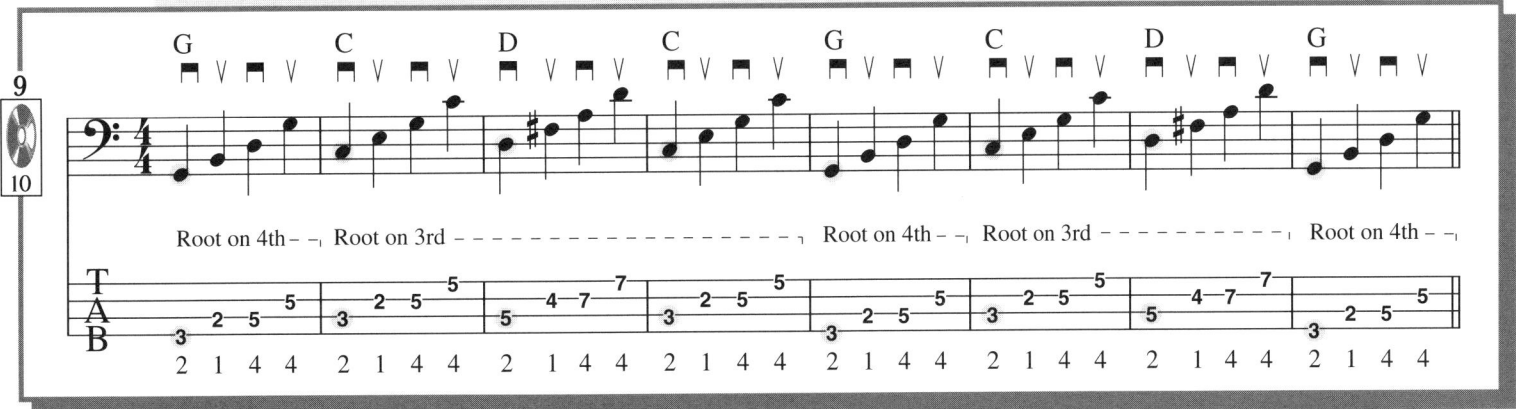

LESSON 6
The Major Scale

Because so much of what we do as both guitarists and bassists is most easily discussed in relation to the *major scale*, it deserves its own lesson. A *scale* is a series of notes arranged in a specific order of *whole steps* (a distance of two frets) and *half steps* (one fret). The major scale, which is the basis for many other scales and of chords, is constructed with the following formula of whole (W) and half (H) steps:

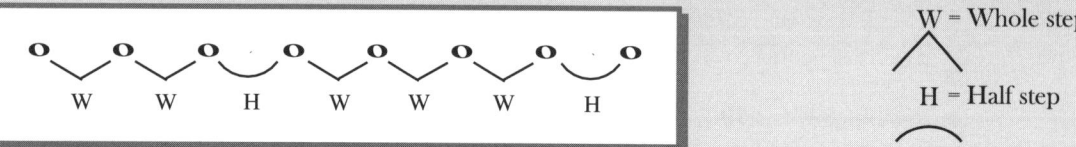

W = Whole step

H = Half step

Here is what happens when this formula is applied to a scale starting on C, which is the *tonic* (often called the *root*) of the scale. The transposable scale pattern shown is very useful and should be memorized. Note that this pattern has the low root on the 3rd string.

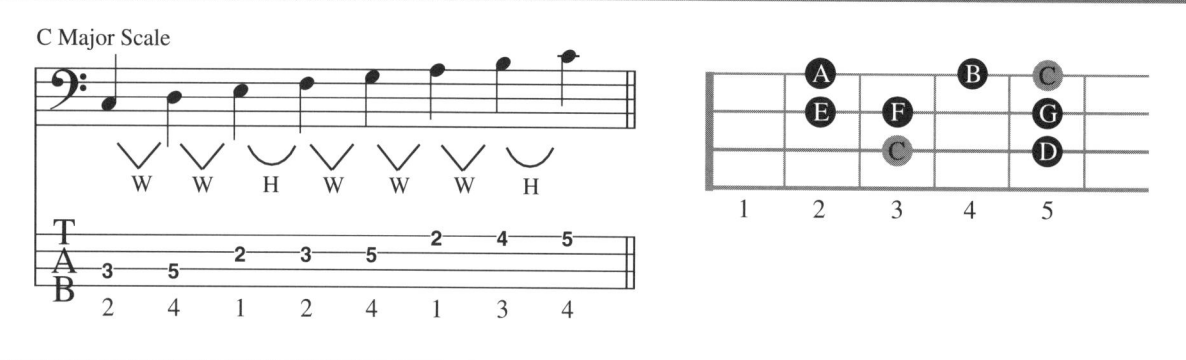

The C Major scale is the only major scale that has no sharps or flats. Any other major scale will either have sharps or flats (never both!). Below is the G Major scale. Notice that it has one sharp (F♯), and that although the scale pattern has the root on the 4th string, it is identical to the pattern for C Major.

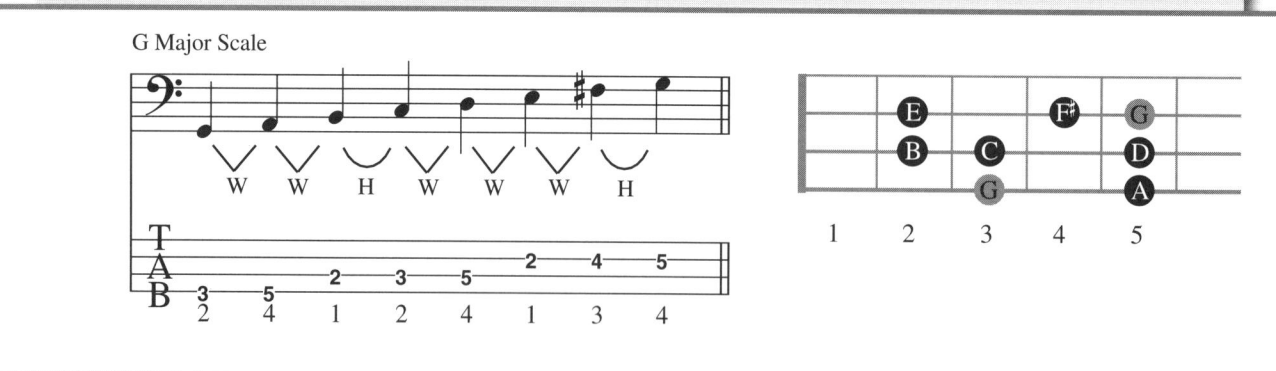

Here is the D Major scale, which has two sharps (F♯ and C♯). Again, although it is a whole step higher than the C Major scale, the pattern is the same.

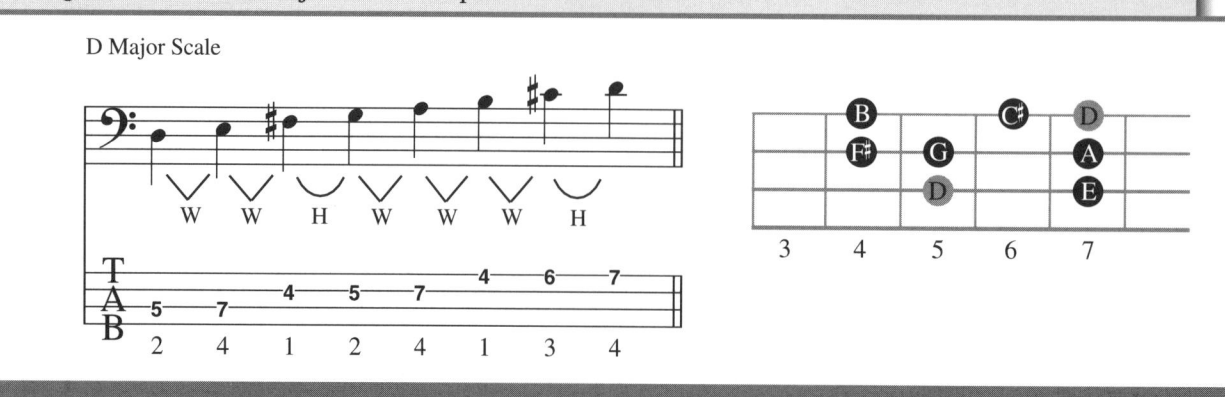

A major scale starting on the 1st fret will have a different pattern. Here is the F Major scale, which has one flat (B♭). This is also a transposable pattern, which means that you can use it to play the C, G and D Major scales, too. Although this scale has the low root on the 4th string, the same pattern will also work if the root is on the 3rd string.

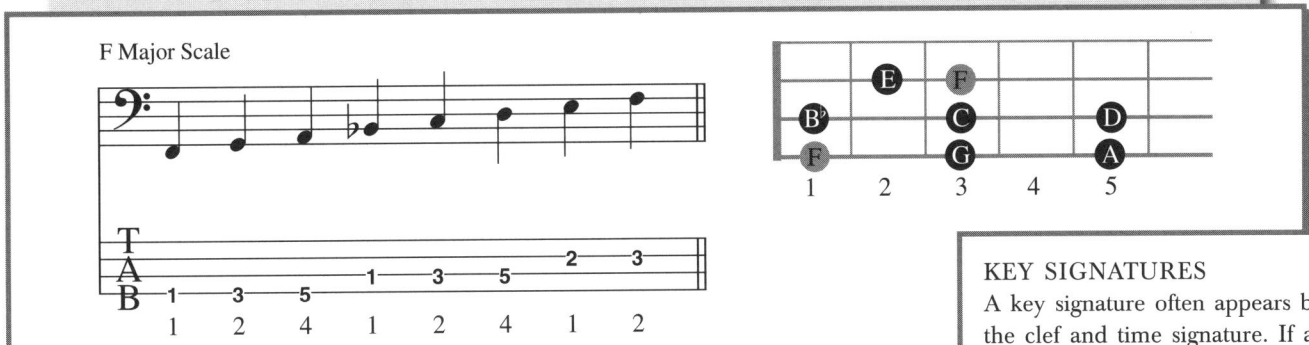

In example 9 on page 11, we used strictly chord tones (notes from the chords) to make a bass line. Lines such as these, where the notes of a chord are played one at a time, are called *arpeggios*. Using the major scale, we can play *stepwise* or *scaler* lines (lines that move mostly in whole and half steps). Below is a mostly stepwise line for the same progression in example 9 using the G Major scale. Notice that the roots of the chords are still reinforced on the downbeats.

KEY SIGNATURES
A key signature often appears between the clef and time signature. If an accidental appears on the line or space of a note, that note is sharp or flat throughout the piece in all octaves (unless marked with a natural sign). If you know the major scales and the key signature has one sharp (F♯), you will know the piece uses the G Major scale and is therefore in the key of G Major.

Key signature

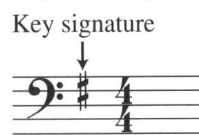

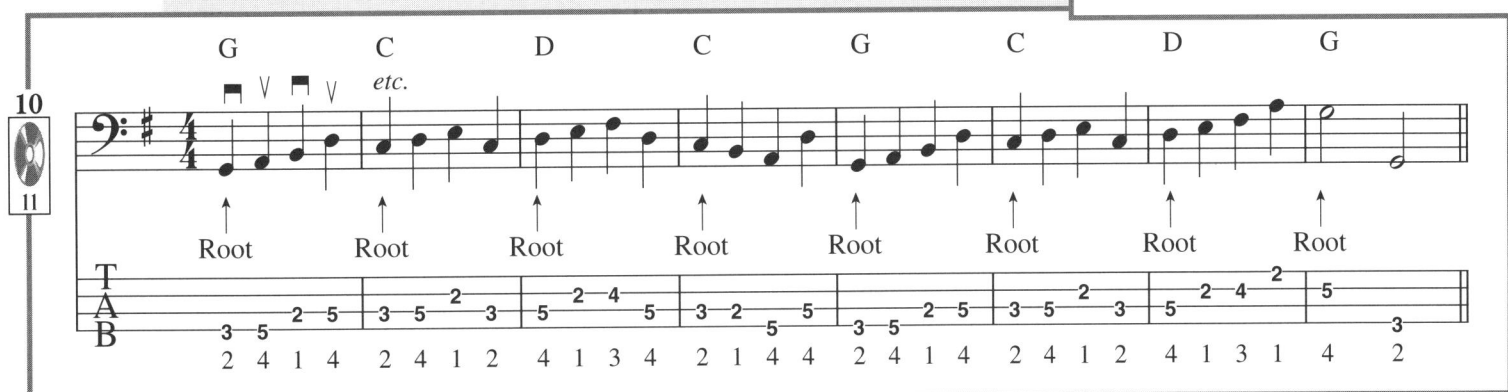

Here is a major scale warmup in D Major. This is a great way to start a practice session. Notice that the first eight bars (measures) have a four-note pattern that is *sequenced* (repeated on a different pitch level), descending from high D. In the next eight bars, the pattern is sequenced ascending back to the high D. (If you learn the finger pattern thoroughly, you can transpose this to any key just by starting on a different fret.)

LESSON 7
Major and Minor Triads

On pages 10 and 11 you learned two patterns for playing arpeggio bass lines with major chords. Now that you know about the major scale, you can have a better understanding of those patterns.

A triad is a three-note chord made with the root, third and fifth notes of a major scale. As you learned on pages 10 and 11, these notes are often repeated (doubled) to play a chord on the guitar. This example shows how a major triad is made from a major scale.

Here is a C Major arpeggio like those you played on page 11. Notice that each chord tone is given a name: root, 3rd or 5th.

Another important triad is the minor triad. It is just like the major triad, but the 3rd is lowered by one half step (♭3).

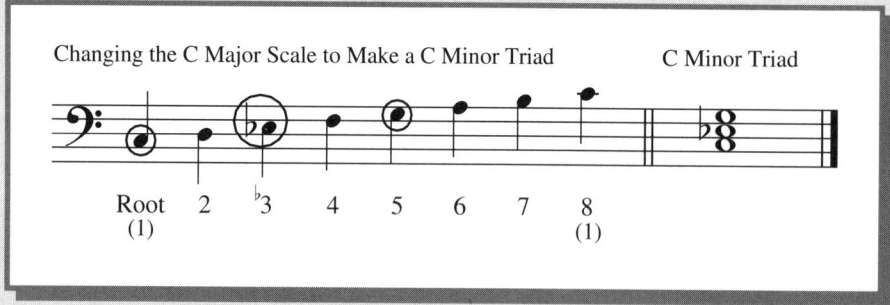

You can change a major triad to minor by using a flat or natural sign to lower the 3rd. A major chord symbol simply shows the name of the root: C Major is C; D Major is D. In this book, a minor chord symbol shows min after the name of the root: C Minor is Cmin; D Minor is Dmin. Other commonly used symbols for minor chords are a lowercase m (Cm) or a minus sign (C-).

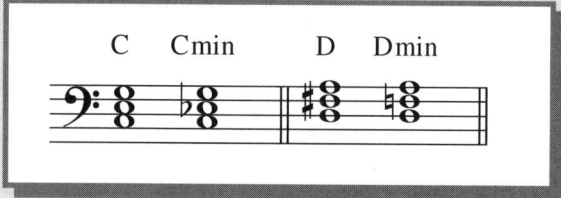

LESSON 8
Playing Bass Lines with Minor Chords

As with major chords (page 10), it is helpful to remember the minor chord forms you play on the guitar and think of how to play them as arpeggios on the bass. Here are the Emin and Amin chords that you probably know and a suggested bass arpeggio pattern for each. Each bass pattern has one added ♭3 note (in parentheses), to help emphasize the minor sound.

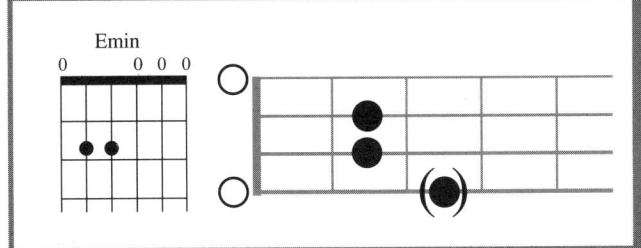

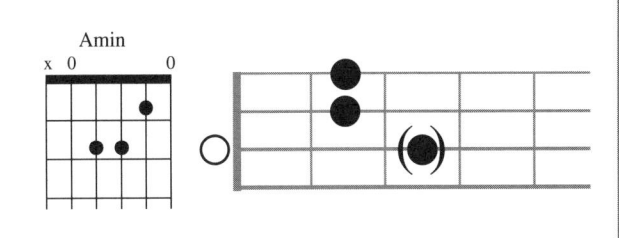

Here is a common two-chord minor chord progression with an arpeggio bass line. Notice the use of the left-facing repeat sign (:‖). When you see this sign, return to the beginning or the closest right-facing repeat sign (‖:) and play the passage again.

Here are some useful transposable patterns to memorize for playing arpeggio bass lines with minor chords.

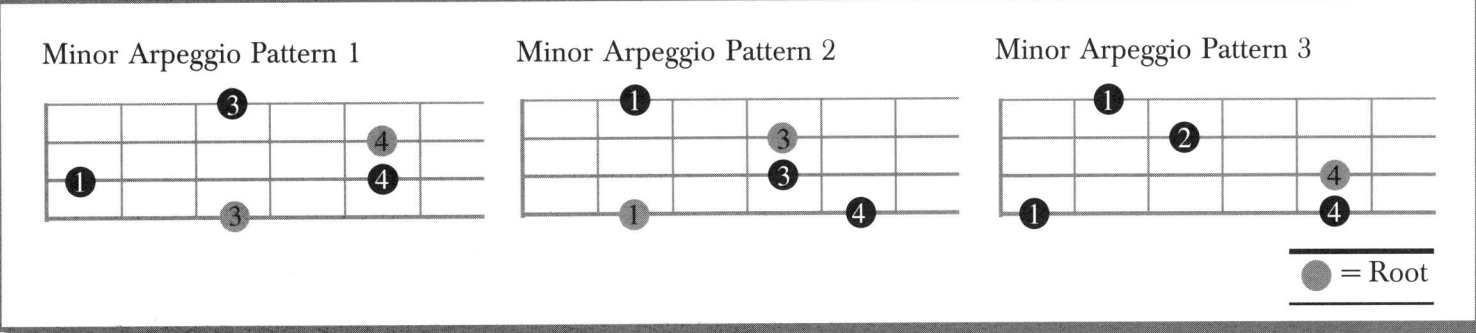

Minor Arpeggio Pattern 1   Minor Arpeggio Pattern 2   Minor Arpeggio Pattern 3

● = Root

Here is a sample chord progression with minor chords and ideas for bass lines. Remember that the patterns you just learned are fully transposable to any root. The patterns being used are labeled in the examples.

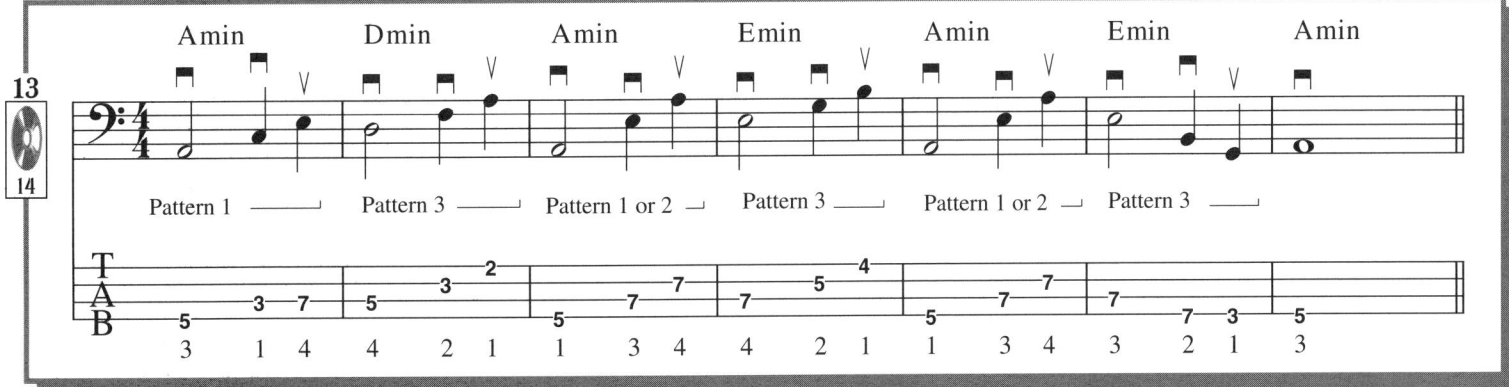

LESSON 9
Reading Eighth Notes, Ties and Dots

EIGHTH NOTES

As you know, as note values get smaller, they halve the duration of the next larger values: A half note is half as long as a whole note; a quarter note is half as long as a half note. We can continue this process with an *eighth note*, which is half as long as a quarter note.

A single eighth note looks like a quarter note (it has a filled head and a stem), except that it also has a flag. Consecutive eighth notes are connected by a *beam*.

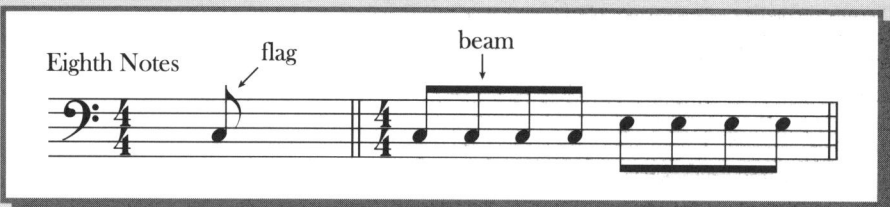

Since an eighth note is half the duration of a quarter note and a quarter note equals one beat, an eighth note equals half a beat. The easiest way to count eighth notes is to divide each beat in half, like this: "1 and, 2 and, 3 and, 4 and, 1 and, 2 and," etc. We will use the ampersand (&) to represent "and." It's easy to understand dividing beats in half if you think about tapping your foot. There are two parts to each beat: foot on the ground (1) and foot off the ground (&).

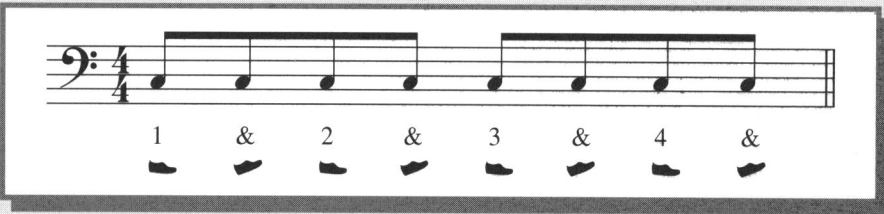

TIES

The length of a note can be extended by connecting it with a tie to another note of the same pitch. The second of two tied notes is not struck. This is most useful when extending a note into a new measure.

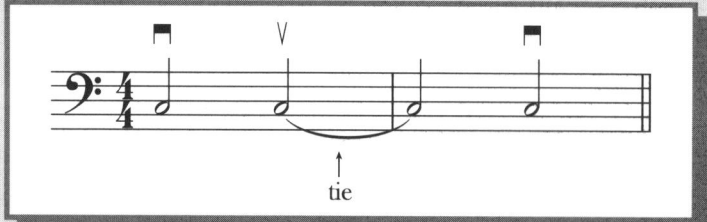

DOTS

Another way to extend the value of a note is with a dot. A dot increases the value of a note by half. For example, a dotted half note is worth three beats: a half note equals two beats (2), half of that is one beat (1) and $2 + 1 = 3$. A dotted half note is like a half note tied to a quarter note. A dotted quarter note is like a quarter note tied to an eighth note (one-and-a-half beats).

LESSON 10
Reading in 2nd Position

On pages 8 and 9, you practiced reading in open position without TAB. Now, it's time to practice reading in 2nd position (mostly on the 2nd, 3rd, 4th and 5th frets). This position is especially good for playing in G Major (one sharp, F♯) and D Major (two sharps, F♯ and C♯), because F♯ and C♯ fall easily under the fingers.

NOTES IN 2ND POSITION

This example combines arpeggios and scales under a typical D Major chord progression. Observe the key signature; all F and C notes are played sharp. It includes eighth notes, so count carefully.

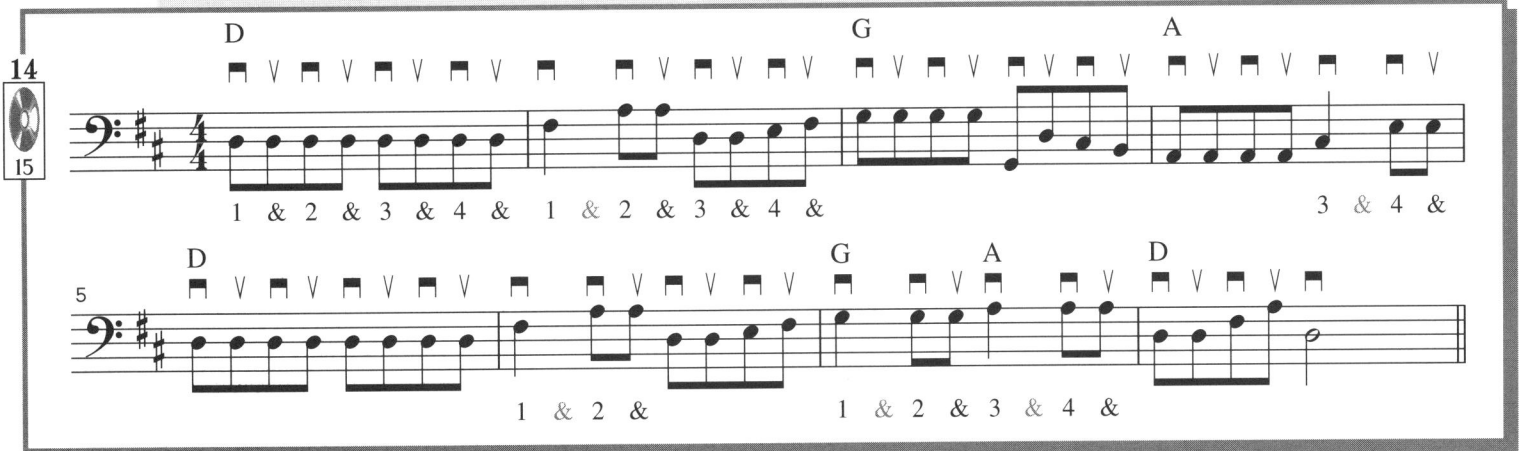

¾ TIME

This example uses a new time signature: ¾. While ¾ is not commonly used in rock and blues, you may come across it on other kinds of gigs, such as reading show tunes or standards. There are three beats per measure, and while everything else is the same, it "feels" quite different. This is the time signature for a waltz. Keep your eye out for dotted notes and ties and notice the key signature, which is G Major (one sharp, F♯). This one is tough and is meant to stretch you a little. You may want to start quite slowly (set the metronome to 48) and count aloud while you practice.

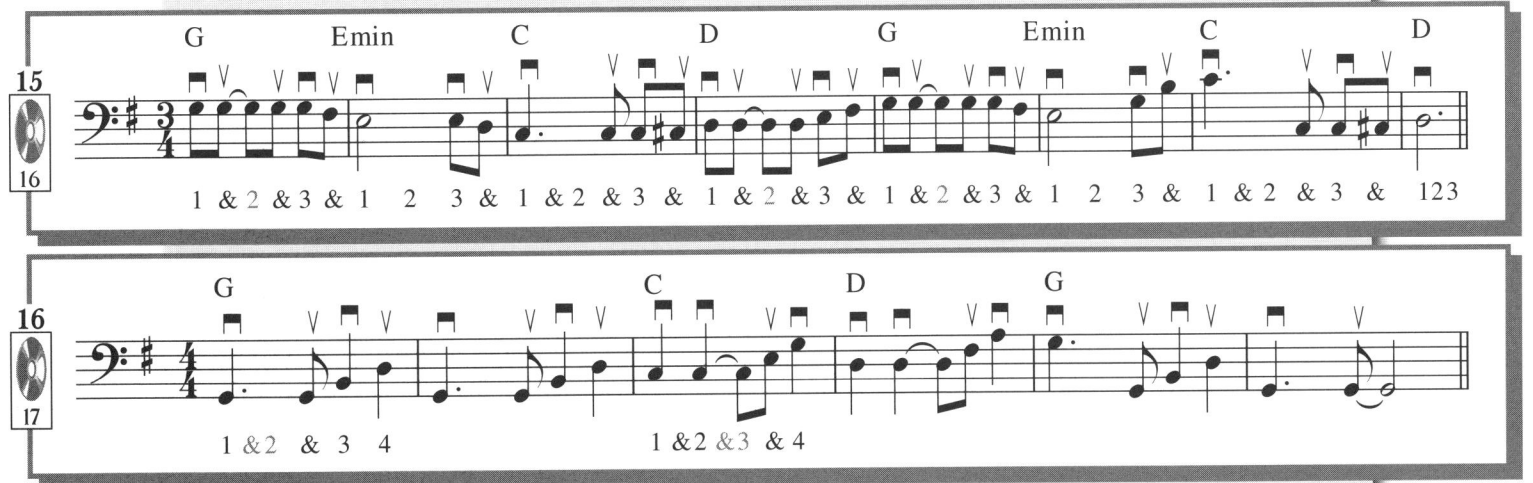

LESSON 11
Rests

A silence is just as important as a note, especially in a bass line. Often, it is the combination of notes and silences that most clearly defines a rhythm.

REST VALUES

Here are the corresponding rest symbols for the note values that we have covered thus far.

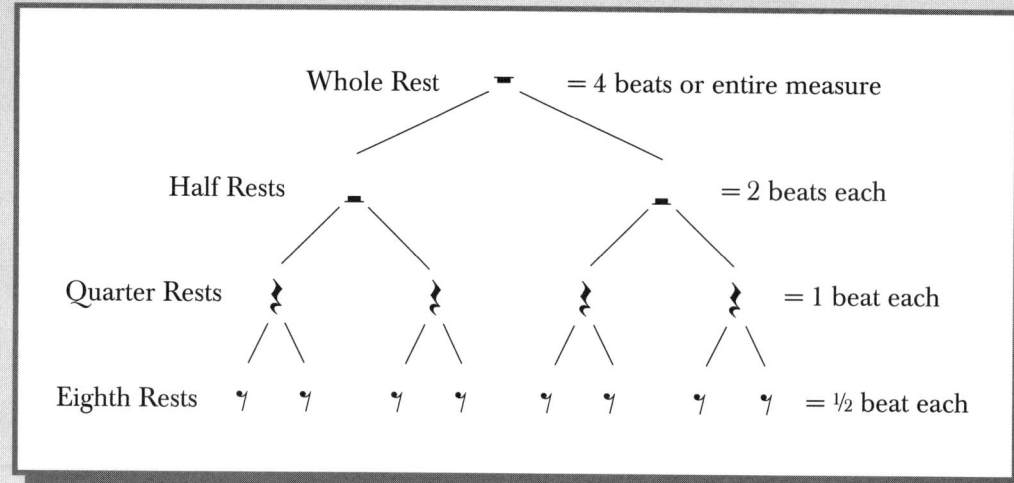

ARTICULATION TECHNIQUE

Articulation refers to how notes are played in respect to other notes; the notes either connect smoothly to one another, with no silence between them, or they are disconnected.

Notes that are smoothly connected are said to be legato. Legato playing is achieved by keeping left-hand fingers securely on their notes until the next one is played and only touching the string with the right-hand fingers when it is time to pluck. In other words, if you remove your left-hand finger from a note before the next is fingered, it will silence the note and cause a disconnection; touching a string with your right hand before plucking will also silence the note cause a disconnection.

In the following exercise, you will get a chance to try both kinds of articulation. In the first bar, keep your 1st finger down at all times, only adding your 3rd finger when it is time to play the 2nd note and being very careful not to touch the string early with the right hand. You should hear no gap between the C and D. In the second bar, intentionally release the pressure from the fretboard with your left hand on the second and fourth beats, keeping the finger on the string to keep it from vibrating. Furthermore, put your right-hand finger (or pick) on the string for beats 2 and 4 to help the left hand dampen or mute the string. You will hear a clear gap between the notes.

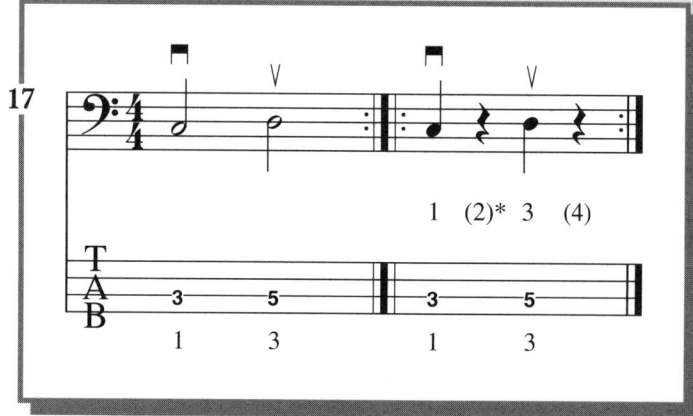

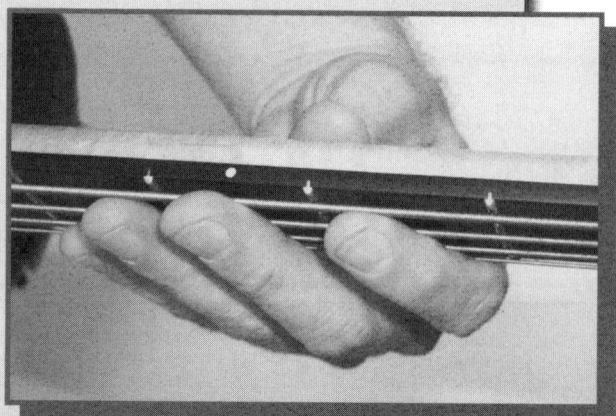

Keep your finger on the string but release it from the fretboard to stop a note.

* Numbers in parenthesis between staff and TAB correspond to rests in music. They are used to assist in counting beats.

BASS LINES WITH RESTS

Following are bass lines that include rests. Use the techniques you learned on page 18 to guarantee silence during the rests.

Notice what a few well-placed rests can do to make a steady stream of eighth notes more interesting.

Think of the parts of the beats that fall on the numbers as onbeats, and the parts on the "ands" as offbeats. An eighth rest on the onbeat, which is considered the strong part of the beat, will shift the emphasis to the offbeat, the weak part of the beat. This is called syncopation. Without syncopation, there would be no funk or jazz.

LESSON 12
Playing Bass Lines with Diminished Chords

The root, lowered 3 (♭3) and lowered 5th (♭5) of a major scale make a diminished triad.

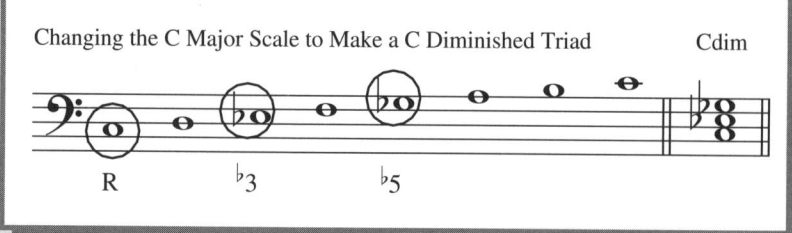

You can change a minor triad to a diminished triad by using a flat or a natural sign to lower the 5th.

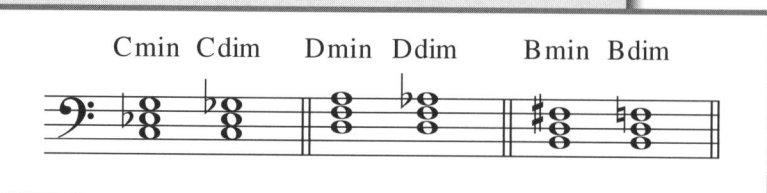

Here are some useful transposable patterns to memorize for playing arpeggio bass lines with diminished chords.

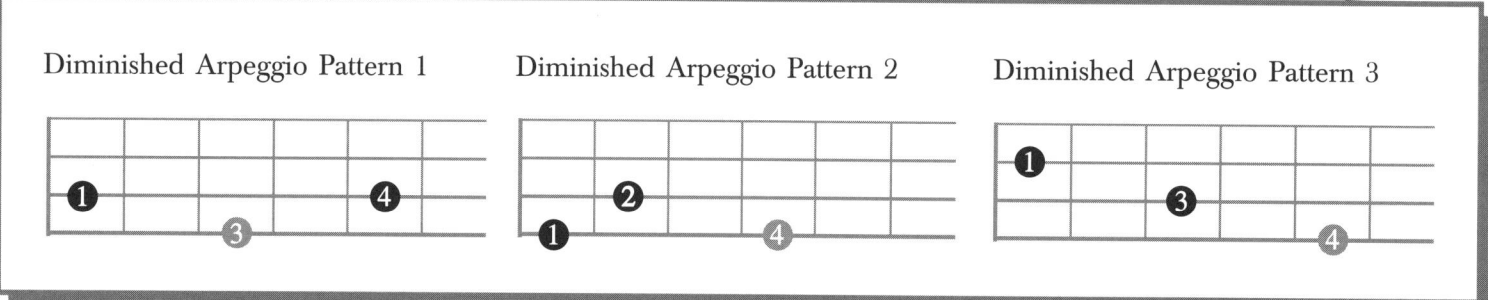

Diminished Arpeggio Pattern 1   Diminished Arpeggio Pattern 2   Diminished Arpeggio Pattern 3

Here is a sample chord progression with diminished chords and ideas for bass lines. Remember that the patterns you just learned are fully transposable to any root. The patterns being used are labeled in the examples.

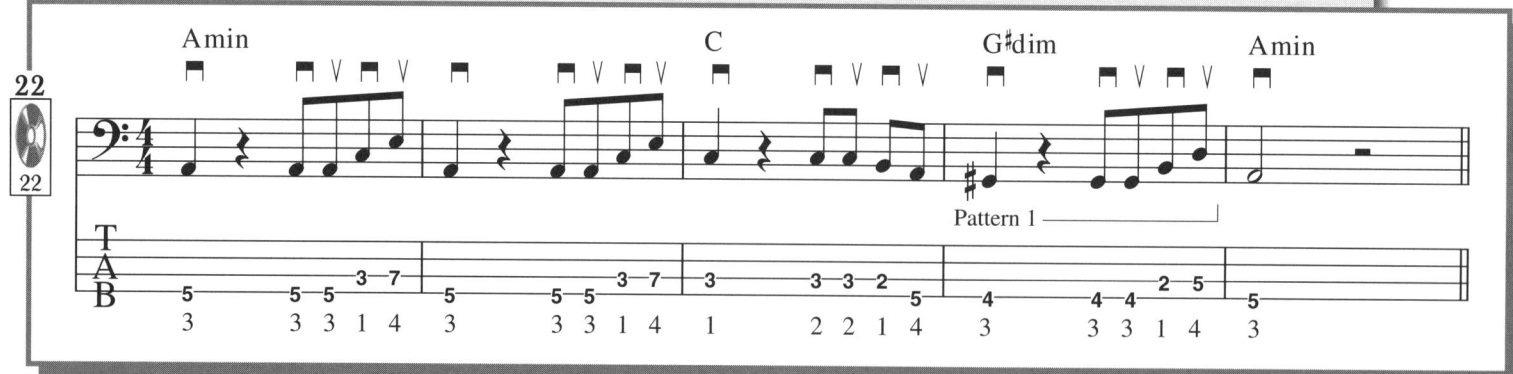

LESSON 13
Playing Bass Lines with Augmented Chords

The root, 3rd and raised 5th (♯5) of a major scale make an augmented triad.

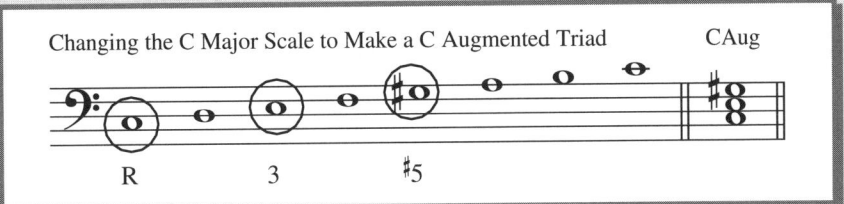

You can change a major triad to an augmented triad by using an accidental to raise the 5th. In most cases, a sharp or a natural sign will do the trick.

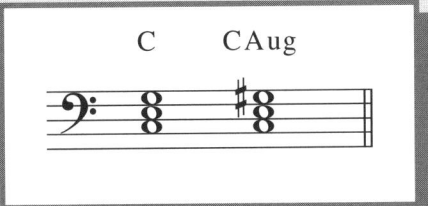

ENHARMONIC EQUIVALENTS
If the 5th is already a sharp note, as in an F♯ Major triad (F♯–A♯–C♯), a *double sharp* sign, ✗, which shows that a note has been raised a whole step, can be used to raise the 5th. C♯ becomes C✗. If you are thinking, "Wait a minute, if I raise a C one whole step, I'll get D," you're right. C✗ and D have the same sound but different names, which means that they are enharmonically equivalent. In order to fit the theoretical rule about using the root, 3rd and 5th of a major scale to make a triad, we need to use C✗ instead of D.

Here are some helpful transposable augmented arpeggio patterns.

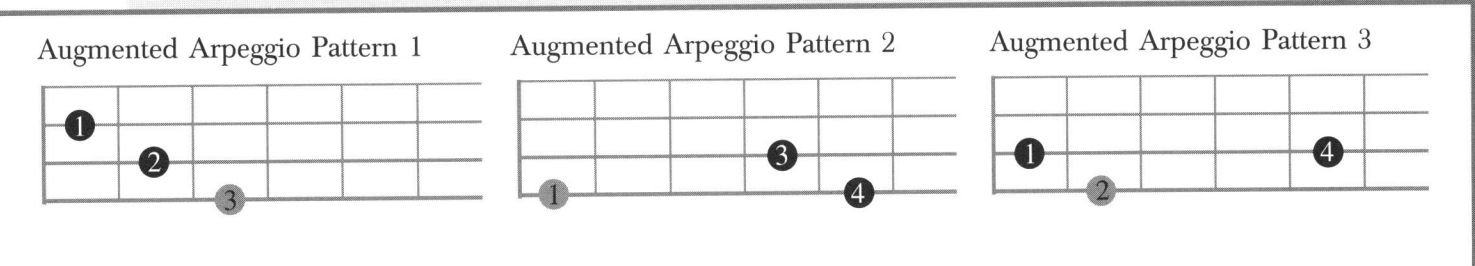

Here is a bass line that includes an augmented arpeggio.

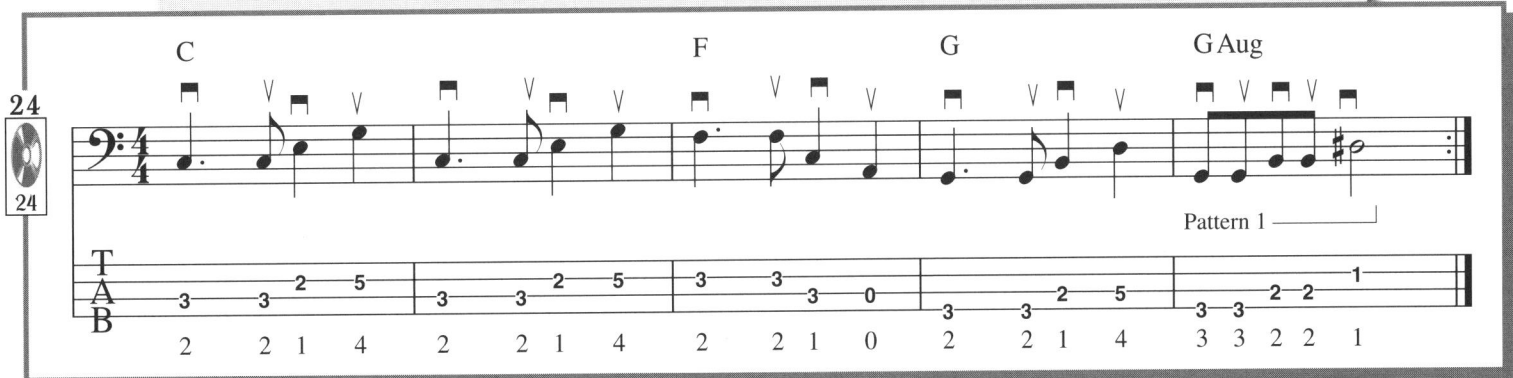

LESSON 14
Reading in 5th Position

THE NOTES IN 5TH POSITION

Below are the notes in the 5th position. The highest note is new; it is a high D♯/E♭ (enharmonic equivalents). There is at least one pair of enharmonic equivalents on each string.

This example will use several different melodic patterns to help become familiar with playing in the 5th position. Before playing, try to say the names of the notes aloud. Strive to become so confident that you can do this in rhythm with a metronome. Once you can do this, you'll be well on your way to being a fluent reader in this region of the fretboard.

Pay close attention to the octaves in this next example. An octave is the closest distance between two different notes with the same name. The 4th string E of your bass is an octave lower than the 6th string E of your guitar. Try to become familiar with the shapes the octaves form on the fretboard. This will be covered in greater depth on page 23.

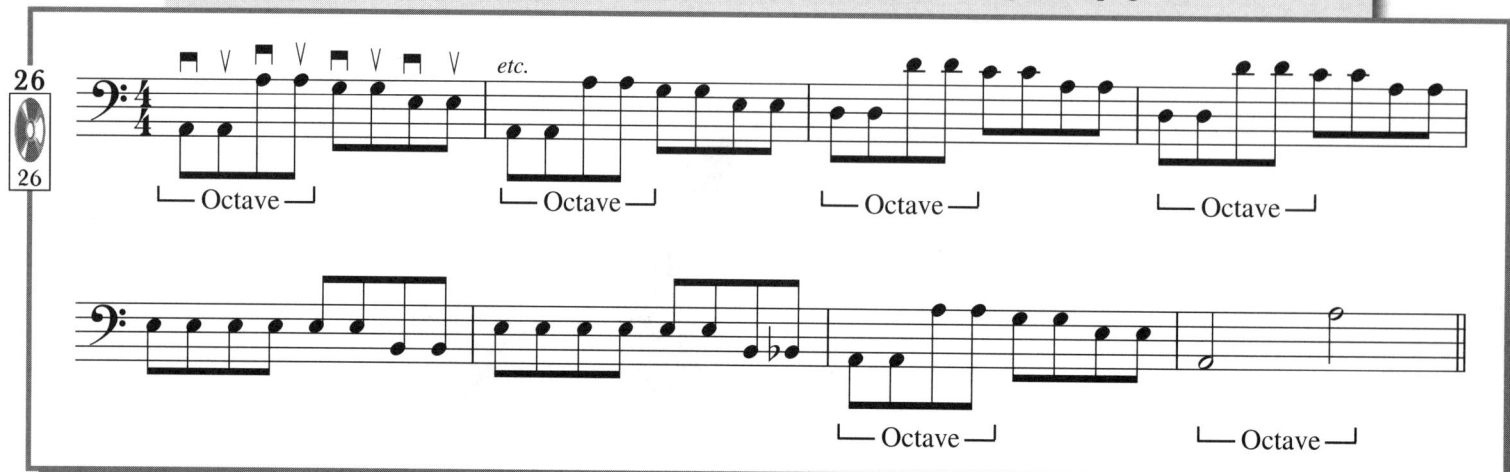

Here is a C Major scale exercise to play in 5th position.

LESSON 15
Notes in Two Positions and Octaves

NOTES IN TWO POSITIONS

Now that you are reading in the 5th position, there are 12 notes that you can play in two places. They are shown below. Practice playing through them very slowly at first, repeating the exercise many times. Do this until you are confident that you have learned both positions for every note, and can play the exercise smoothly at a moderate pace.

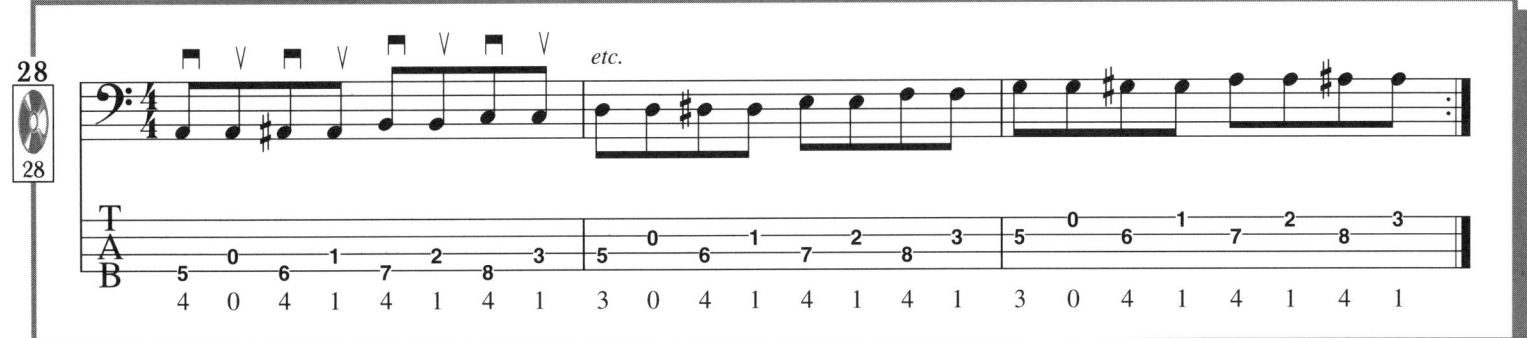

OCTAVES

As mentioned at the bottom of page 22, a bass player should be very aware of the shapes octaves form on the fretboard. This is because they are very useful playing great bass lines. Here are two important octave shapes, followed by a cool octave bass line.

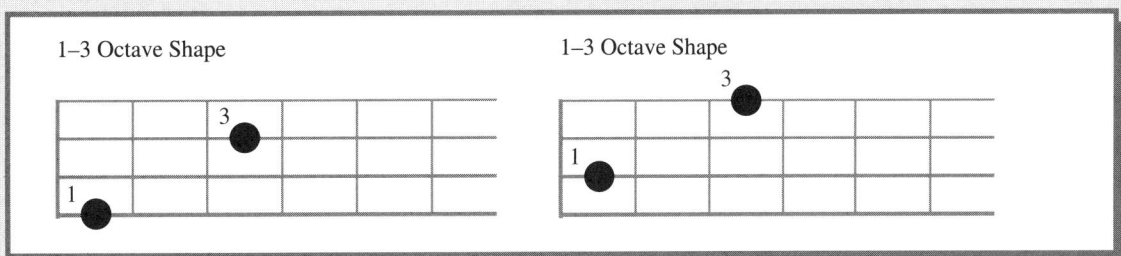

1–3 Octave Shape   1–3 Octave Shape

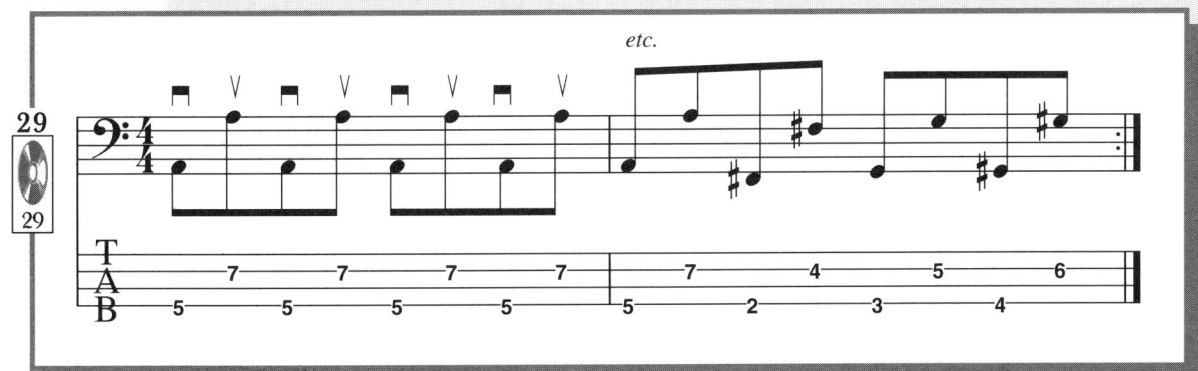

LESSON 16
Diatonic Harmony:
The Triads of the Major Scale

Being ready to fill the bass spot in a band will require you to be ready to play bass lines for many different chord progressions. To be prepared, you will ultimately have to acquaint yourself with a number of standard progressions you might expect to come across. It helps to be able to understand and categorize them. That is where the study of diatonic harmony comes in. Diatonic means "belonging to the scale of the key." Harmony refers to the chords that are within the key. Let's start with the chords of C Major.

DIATONIC TRIADS IN THE KEY OF C MAJOR

If we create a triad on every note in the C Major scale, and do not alter any note with a sharp or flat, we have the diatonic harmonies of the key of C Major. As discussed on page 14, triads are made by stacking every other note of the scale on top of each other to create a three-note chord. Some of the triads will be major, some will be minor and one will be diminished. Uppercase Roman numerals are used to label major chords and lowercase Roman numerals are used for minor and diminished chords. Also, this symbol ○ is used for diminished triads. There is a quick review of Roman numerals at the right.

Roman Numerals		
I .... i		1
II............. ii		2
III............ iii		3
IV .... iv		4
V .... v		5
VI .... vi		6
VII .... vii		7

Note That:
I, IV and V are major
ii, iii and vi are minor
vii○ is diminished

The sequence is the same in every key.

DIATONIC TRIADS IN THE KEY OF G MAJOR

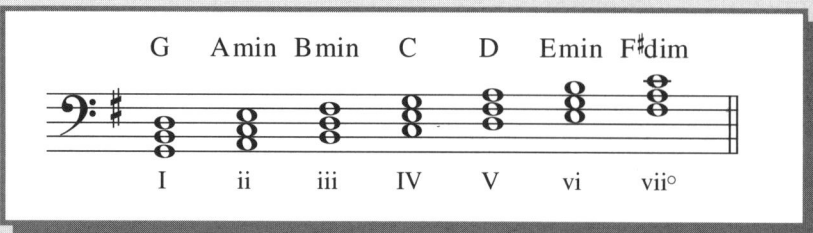

Here are exercises for playing arpeggios of the diatonic triads in several keys. You can review arpeggios for major, minor and diminished chords on pages 11, 15 and 20, respectively.

DIATONIC ARPEGGIOS IN THE KEY OF C

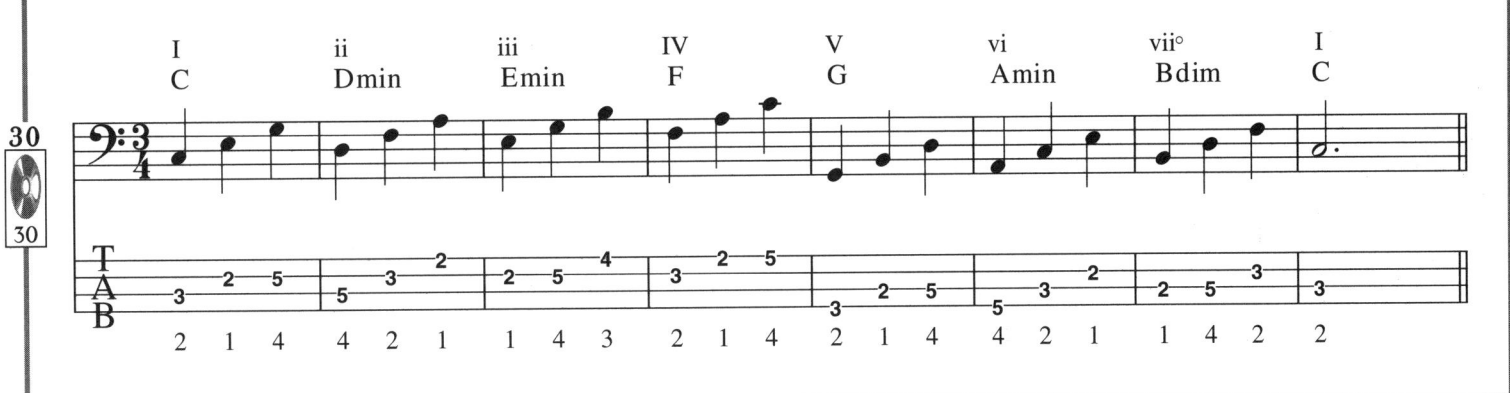

DIATONIC ARPEGGIOS IN THE KEY OF G

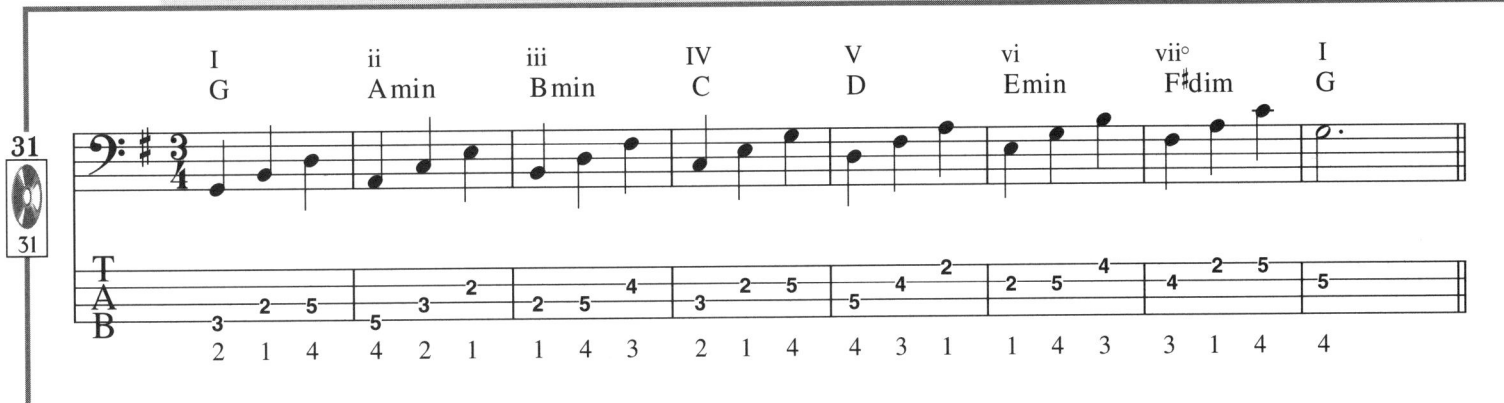

DIATONIC ARPEGGIOS IN THE KEY OF F

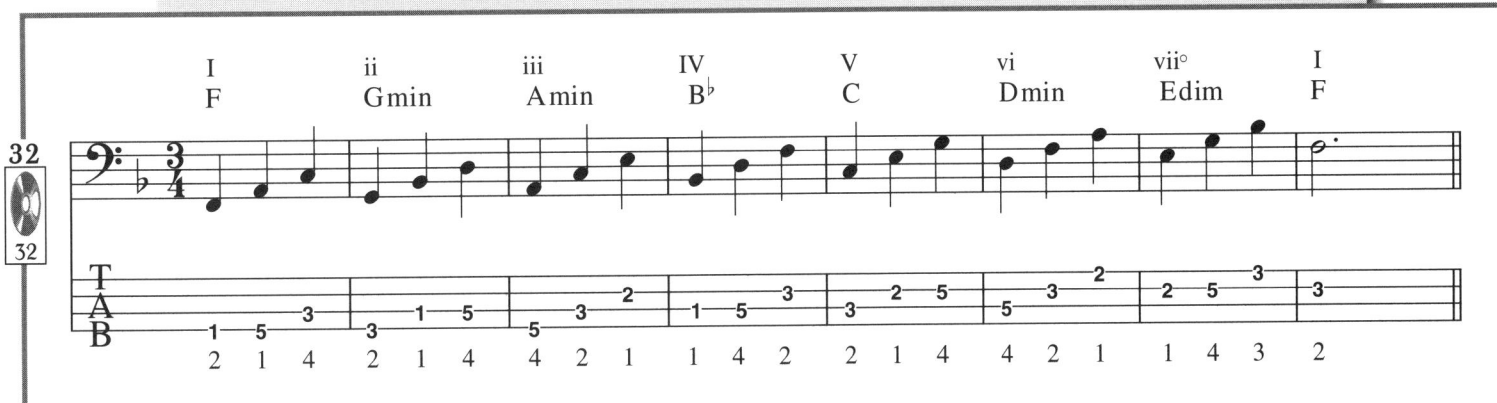

This is a very important part of preparing to be a good bass player. Be sure to go through this procedure with every scale that you learn: learn the diatonic harmonies and then practice arpeggiating them.

LESSON 17
The I–IV–V Progression

On page 24 we briefly discussed how a bass player must be prepared to play bass lines for certain standard chord progressions. The I–IV–V progression is perhaps the most commonly used of all of the standard chord progressions. These three chords, often called the primary chords, are the defining harmonies of a key. In other words, when we hear a I–IV–V, progression, particularly when followed by another I chord (I–IV–V–I) the key of the I chord is established in our ears. Learning to hear and identify chord progressions such as this is an essential skill for any musician. Book and CD kits such as *Ear-Training for the Contemporary Guitarist* by Guy Capuzzo (Alfred #16755) and *Musicianship for the Contemporary Bassist* by Tracy Walton (Alfred #21912), both from the National Guitar Workshop, can help you acquire this skill.

For now, the best thing you can do is bite the bullet and play through the I–IV–V–I progressions in the following arpeggio exercises. Some of them are in new keys, so be sure to be mindful of the key signatures.

C Major

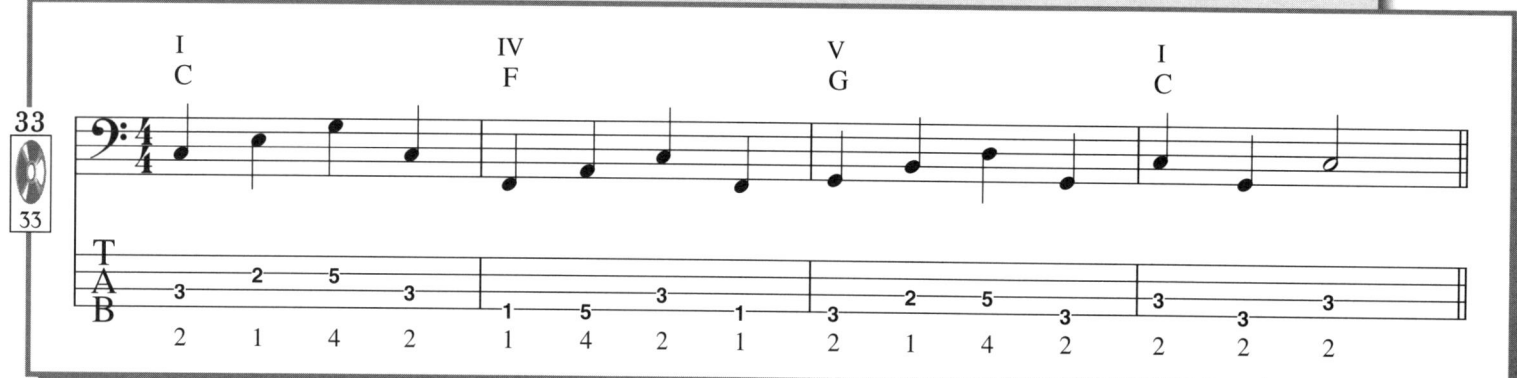

G Major

D Major

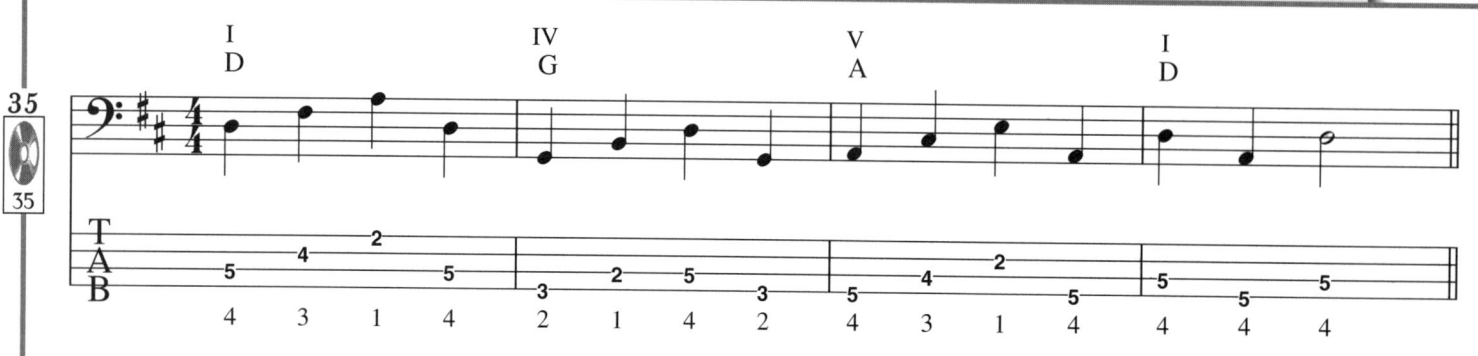

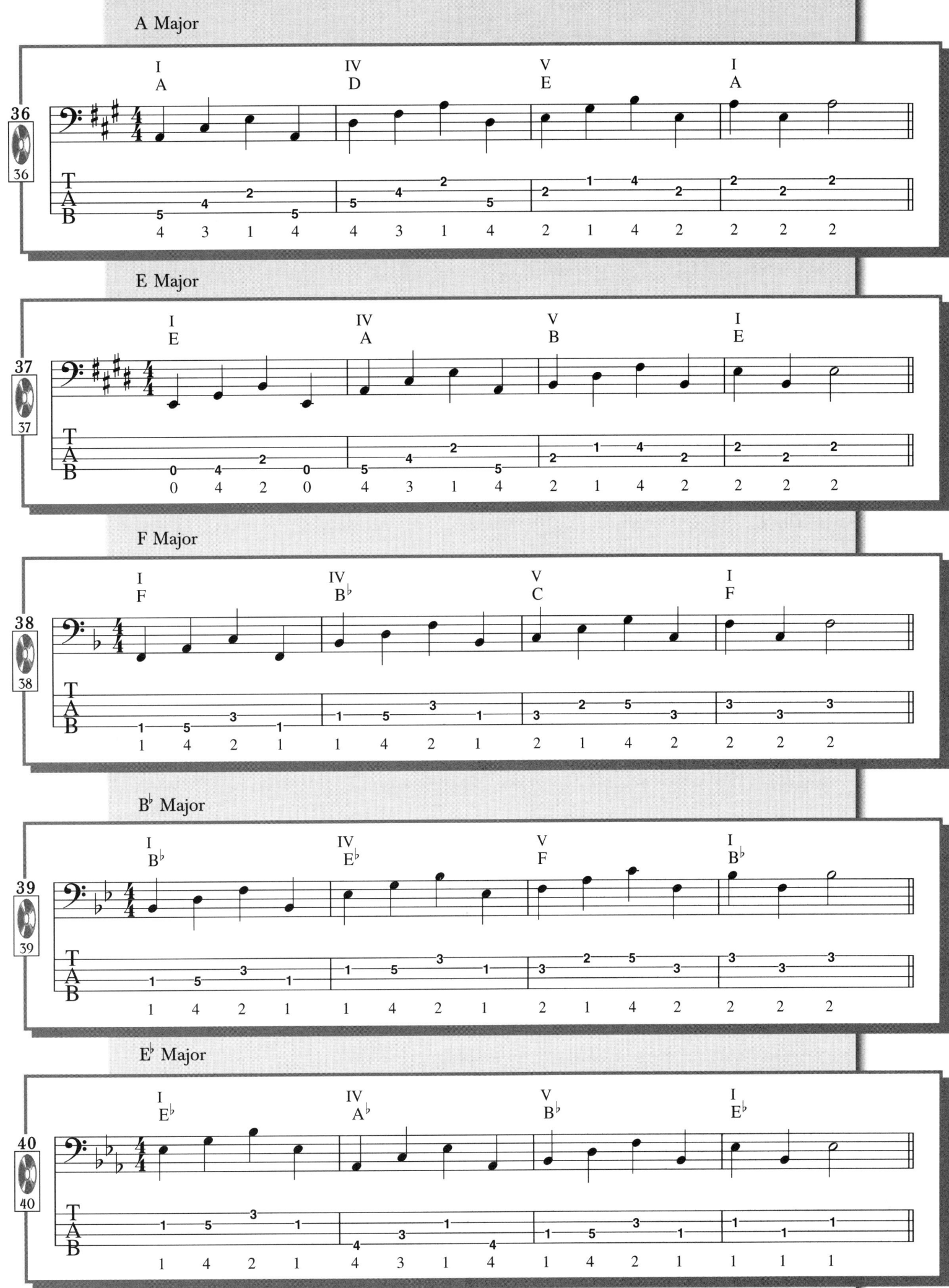

LESSON 18
Hammer-Ons and Pull-Offs

Hammer-ons and pull-offs are the same on the bass as on the guitar, so this is another aspect of picking up the bass that will be easy for you. Physically, the techniques will feel a little different because of the wider spacing of the frets and the thicker strings. Otherwise, they are the same.

These techniques are used far less often on the bass. As guitarists, we use these techniques for two reasons:

- To create legato (smooth, connected) lines—Only the first note is plucked; the other notes are sounded by the left hand. As a result, they sound very fluid.

- For speed—One can use hammer-ons and pull-offs to play rapid lines without the need for perfect coordination between the left and right hands. Even if you aren't the fastest picker around, these techniques can allow you to play quickly.

While both of those statements are true for playing the bass, too, in many contexts, they don't apply. Since so much of what we do on the bass has to do with laying down the groove, we usually want to hear each note solidly articulated. Speed is usually the domain of the lead guitar player, and often would not help lay down a groove.

All of that being said, there are times when a touch of legato can help a bass line. It is worth checking in with your hammer-on and pull-off chops, just to make sure they're working for your bass playing. We'll also take a look at some examples of how to use them.

HAMMER-ONS

As on the guitar, a hammer-on is an ascending legato executed by plucking a note and driving a left-hand finger down onto the string, sounding the new note without using the right hand. We can perform hammer-ons from open strings or fretted notes, and we can perform multiple hammer-ons from one plucked note. As on the guitar, hammer-ons are indicated with a slur between ascending notes. In this book, you'll also see an "H" above the slurred notes in the TAB.

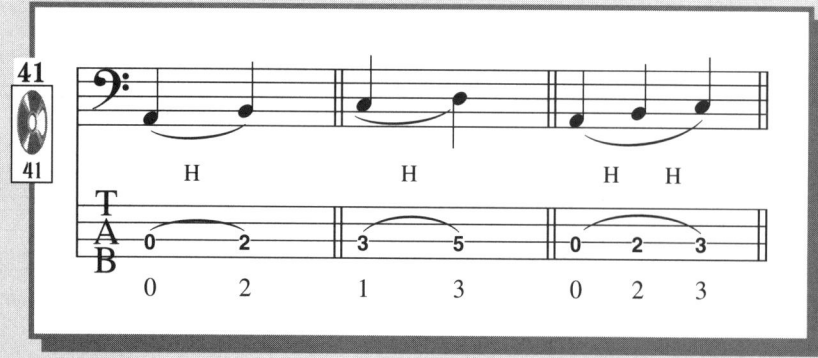

PULL-OFFS

A pull-off is a descending legato executed by plucking a note and snapping a left-hand finger away and down from the string, sounding the new note without using the right hand. We can perform pull-offs from higher fretted notes to lower fretted notes or open strings, and we can perform multiple pull-offs from one plucked note. When pulling-off from one fretted note to another, it is best to put all of the fingers involved down together before plucking. As on the guitar, pull-offs are indicated with a slur between descending notes. In this book, you'll also see a "PO" above the slurred notes in the TAB.

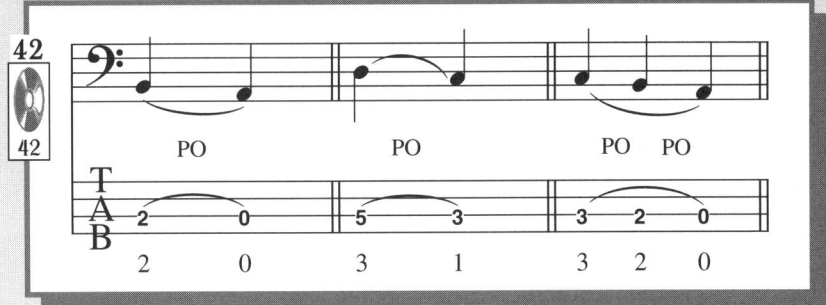

BASS LINES WITH HAMMER-ONS AND PULL-OFFS

Here are some examples of bass lines using these legato techniques. Be careful—it's easy to rush the rhythm of slurred notes. It is a good idea to set your metronome to click eighth notes for part of your practice, and be careful to place your eighth notes directly on the clicks.

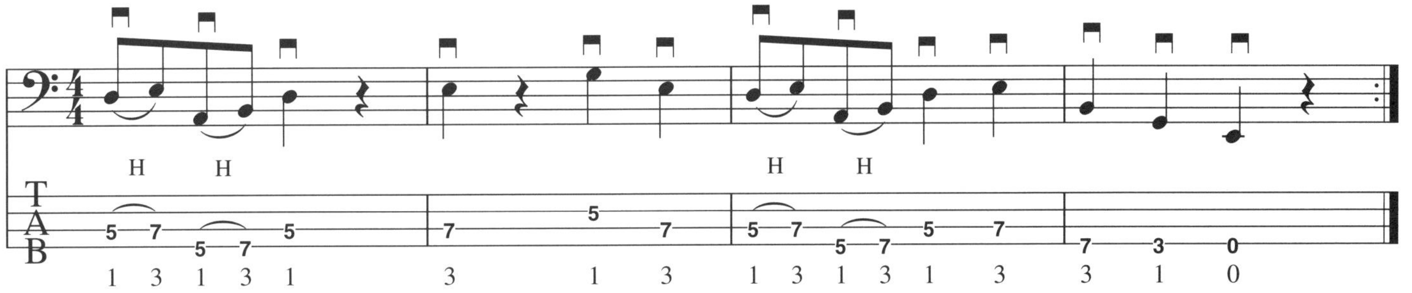

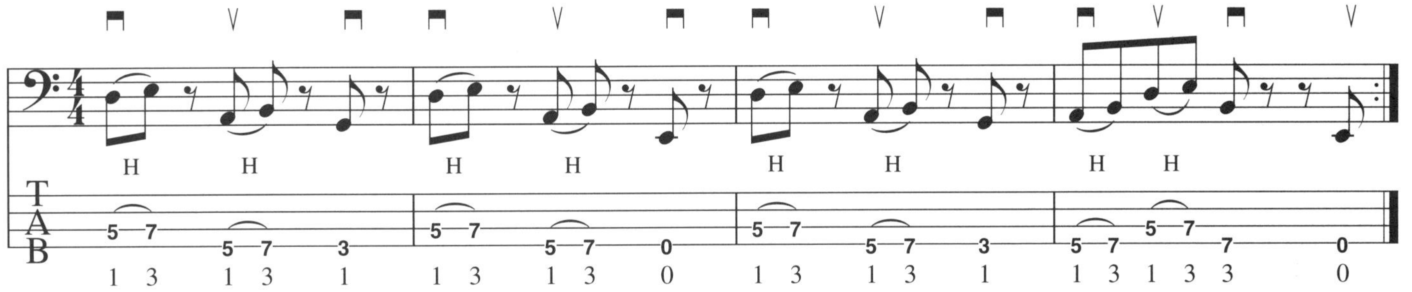

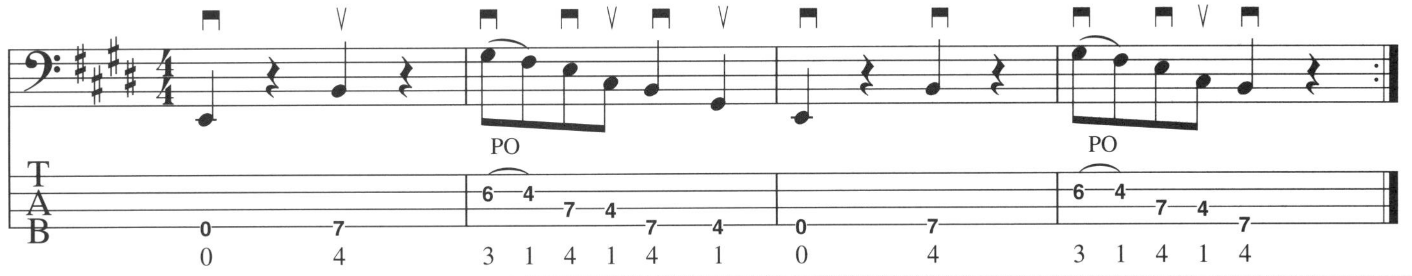

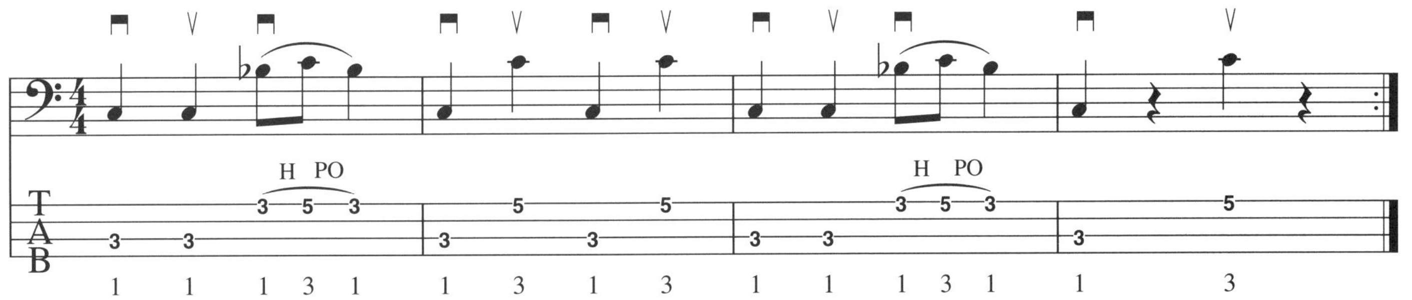

LESSON 19
Sixteenth Notes

As you probably know from your guitar studies, a sixteenth note is ¼ of a quarter note. When a quarter note gets one beat, each beat is divisible by four sixteenth notes. In $\frac{4}{4}$ time, the most common time signature, there are 16 sixteenth notes in a measure (hence the name).

Double Flags

The example to the right is an individual sixteenth note along with its corresponding sixteenth rest. Notice how both have a double flag. The best way to count sixteenth notes is shown below. Notice that consecutive sixteenth notes are connected with double beams.

Following are a few easy exercises to help you become comfortable counting and playing sixteenth notes. Here's an important practice tip: Before playing each example, count aloud and clap the rhythm. This will help your confidence and make playing easier and more fun.

Note that when both eighth and sixteenth notes occur within a single beat, they share a beam. The single beam is the eighth note, the double beams are the sixteenths.

LESSON 20
Reading Sixteenths Through 7th Position

This would be a good time to review the notes you have learned to read through the 5th position (pages 16, 17 and 22). Here are the notes in 7th position.

Here are some funk-oriented bass lines using sixteenth notes and rests. The counting will not be provided under the music, as on page 30, but you should continue to practice counting aloud before and while playing. Also, be mindful of the key signatures, as you may not be accustomed to reading in them without TAB. Finally, you may have already noticed that these lines, or portions of them, can be played in positions other than the 7th position. Go ahead! Read these in as many positions as you can, and don't be afraid to experiment with mixing the positions. Have a blast.

This one is not a funk line. It is a pattern-based major scale exercise. This area of the bass fretboard lends itself well to E Major. Also, pattern recognition is an important part of being a good sight-reader.

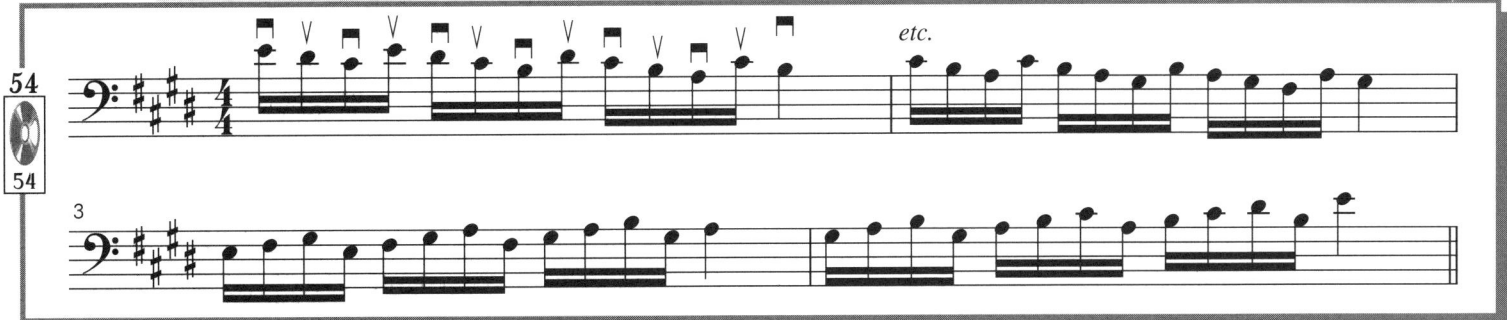

LESSON 21
7th Chords

A 7th chord is a four-note chord that includes a triad and an added note a 7th above the root. Likely, you play them all the time on the guitar. From a bass player's perspective, four-note chords are more fun than triads because the additional note makes for more interesting arpeggios.

To play arpeggio bass lines under 7th chords, you will need to know their formulas. Just in case you haven't learned them already in your guitar studies, here's a chart showing four different types of 7th chords (built on a C root) and their formulas.

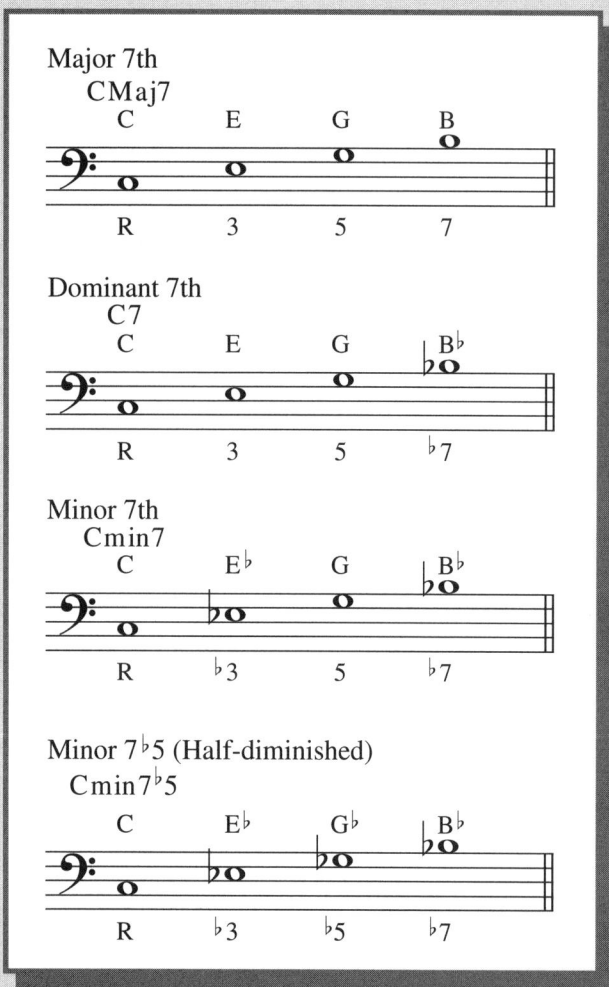

The most commonly used 7th chord is the dominant 7th. This chord is especially useful in the blues. Each 7th chord correlates with a scale that can be used to create bass lines for that chord. The dominant 7th chord correlates to the Mixolydian mode, which is the scale that is created when a major scale is played beginning and ending on the 5th degree. For example, if you play a C Major scale beginning and ending on G, you've got the G Mixolydian mode, which is like a G Major scale with the 7th degree lowered one half step ($\flat$7).

Below is the G Mixolydian mode and the G Dominant 7th chord (G7).

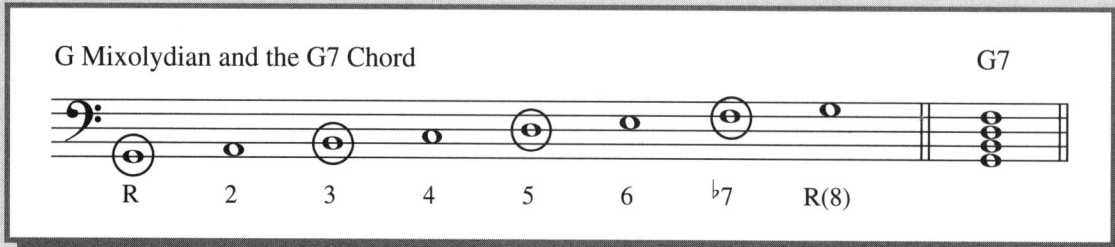

Here are three fingerings for dominant 7th chord arpeggios.

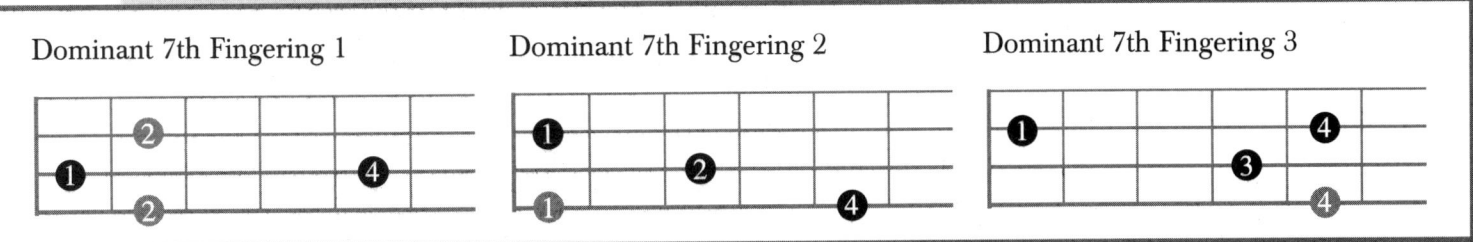

Dominant 7th Fingering 1   Dominant 7th Fingering 2   Dominant 7th Fingering 3

Here are the 12 dominant 7th chords. Play through them all. If necessary, refer to the chart on page 3 to find the notes on the fretboard.

Chord	Notes			
C7	C	E	G	B♭
G7	G	B	D	F
D7	D	F♯	A	C
A7	A	C♯	E	G
E7	E	G♯	B	D
B7	B	F♯	D♯	A
F♯7	F♯	A♯	C♯	E

Chord	Notes			
F7	F	A	C	E♭
B♭7	B♭	D	F	A♭
E♭7	E♭	G	B♭	D♭
A♭7	A♭	C	E♭	G♭
D♭7	D♭	F	A♭	C♭
G♭7	G♭	B♭	D♭	F♭

This example has a very common dominant-chord bass pattern used on thousands of recordings of blues and rock music.

Learning the dominant 7th chord will get you pretty far with basic blues and rock music. It is very important that you learn all of the 7th chords well. See *Beginning Electric Bass* by David Overthrow for a thorough study of the subject, or take the time to find fingerings for all of the chords listed above.

LESSON 22
The 12-Bar Blues

The blues is a style of music born out of early African-American culture that in turn gave birth to rock 'n' roll. It also deeply affected the development of jazz. Blues roots run so deep through so many styles of contemporary music that there is literally no way to be a good musician without at some point digging into the style.

MAJOR BLUES

The blues is also a form. When a bandleader calls out "Blues in E," any musician worth their salt knows what to do: play major or dominant chords through the 12-bar form. It's likely that you have already played lots of blues on the guitar (whether you know it at the time or not), so the only thing new for you may be your role: supporting the groove and the harmony. While the lead guitarist is wailin' and bending, you've got be laying down the groove and clearly outlining the 12-bar blues form. Here's a quick review of the basic blues form:

Chord:	I	I	I	I	IV	IV	I	I	V	IV	I	I
Bar:	1	2	3	4	5	6	7	8	9	10	11	12

Since nearly all blues tunes have more than one chorus (occurrence of the 12-bar progression), the turnaround (last four bars) usually ends on V, which makes us feel like we need to hear I again, thus bringing us around to the top (beginning) of the form again.

Chord:	I	I	I	I	IV	IV	I	I	V	IV	I	V
Bar:	1	2	3	4	5	6	7	8	9	10	11	12

Turnaround _____

There are many variations on the blues turnaround. Below is an important jazz-influenced turnaround Also notice the IV chord in bar 2, this is a common variation on the form and is called a "quick four."

Chord:	I	IV	I	I	IV	IV	I	I	ii	V	I	V
Bar:	1	2	3	4	5	6	7	8	9	10	11	12

Turnaround _____

Here is a standard 12-bar blues bass line.

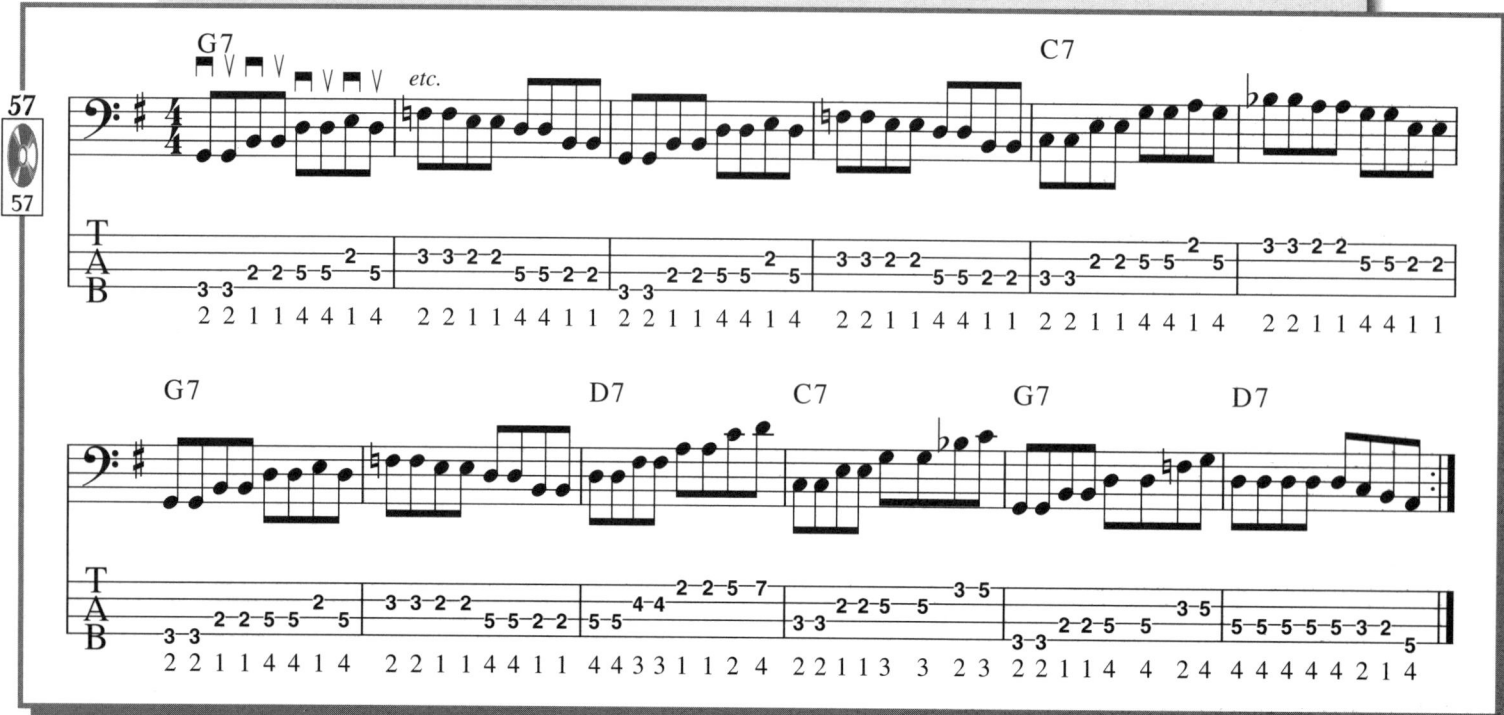

SWING FEEL

Much of rock, blues and jazz music is played with a swing or shuffle feel. You may have done this already without even thinking about it. In swing feel, the eighth notes are played unevenly, long-short, long-short.

The easiest way to understand swing feel is to first consider eighth-note triplets. A triplet is three notes played in the time of two. In an eighth-note triplet, three eighth notes are played in the time of two; in other words, one beat is divided into three equal eighth notes.

Although the eighth notes in swing feel are written as regular, straight eighth notes, they sound like triplets with the first two eighth notes tied.

These are often called swing 8ths. Try the 12-bar blues on page 34 in swing 8ths. In fact, you can go back to any bass line with eighth notes in this book and play it in swing 8ths. Listen for this sound in your favorite blues or rock-blues recordings.

MINOR BLUES

If the bandleader calls out, "Minor blues in A," we must also immediately know what to do. A minor blues can either have a minor v or a major/dominant V. It won't hurt to ask which the bandleader has in mind. Or, just play the root in bar 9 until you hear whether the guitarist (and/or keyboard player) is playing a major or minor chord.

Here is a minor blues bass line. Notice the quick four and the dominant V chord. Play this in swing 8ths.

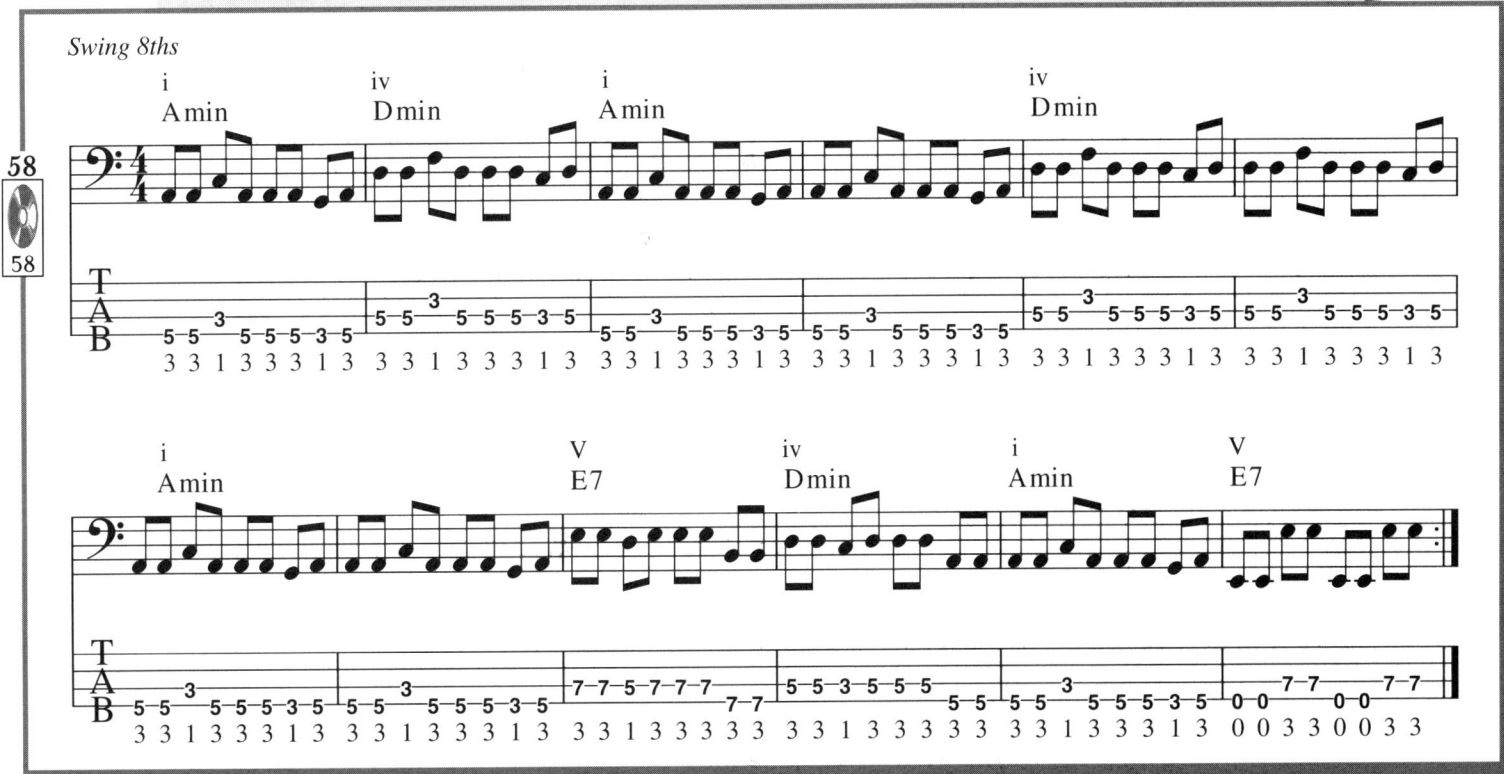

THE ROLE OF THE BASS PLAYER:
PART 2—LOCKING-IN WITH THE DRUMS

Various comments have been made throughout this book about supporting what the drummer is doing, or laying down the groove. This is one of the most important jobs you will have a bass player, and it is entirely different from what you are used to doing as a guitarist.

As a guitarist, you either provide an aspect of the overall rhythm and harmony or you are creating an interesting and exciting solo. As a bassist, you are part of the foundation of the rhythm. The overall feel of the entire rhythm is built on two primary elements: the bass drum (often called "the kick") and the bass guitar.

You must learn to listen to the band. Think of it as a powerful driving machine: you are trying to find the driver's seat so that you can drop into it and move the music forward. Start by listening for what the drummer is doing with the bass drum. In rehearsals, ask him/her to play the drumbeat alone, and focus on the kick. At first, try to create a bass line that is an exact duplicate of the bass-drum rhythm. Hopefully, all of your practice with the metronome will pay off and you will be able to play exactly with the drummer.

We will look at this process by comparing bass lines that don't lock-in so well with bass lines that do. First, you will have to familiarize yourself with basic drum set notation.

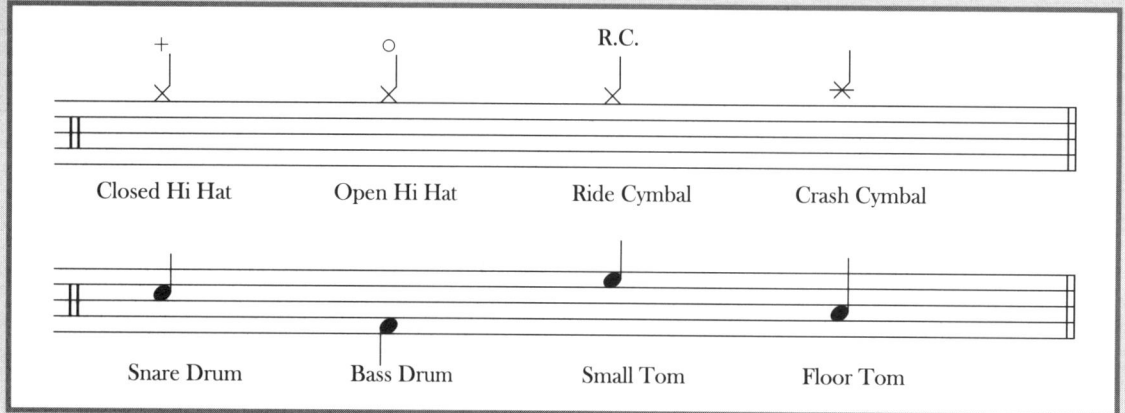

Here is a basic rock backbeat rhythm. A backbeat is one where the accent is on beats 2 and 4. Notice that while the hi-hat provides a constant eighth-note pulse, the bass drum plays on beats 1 and 3 while the snare hits the accents on beats 2 and 4.

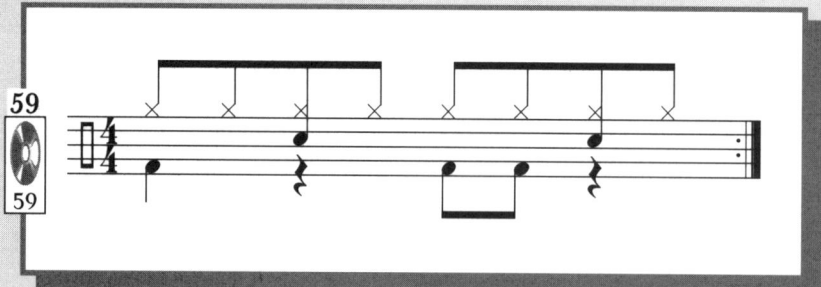

This bass line will fit with the music, but it doesn't lock in very well.

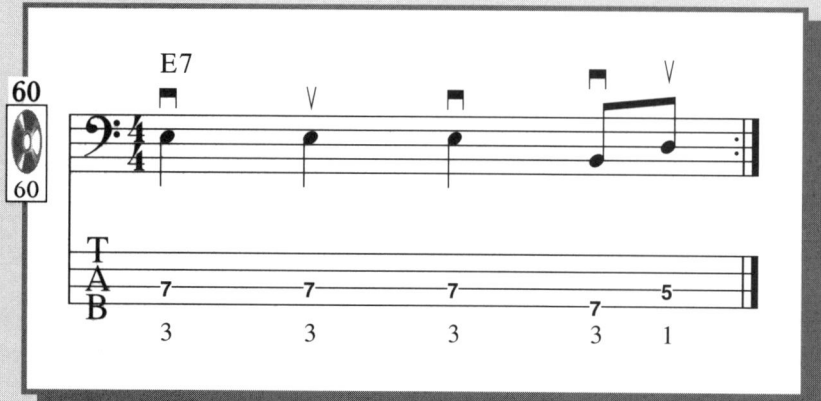

This bass line locks-in beautifully.

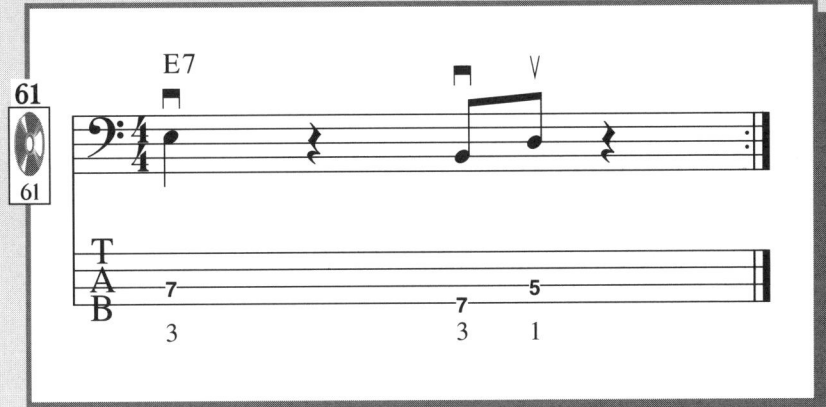

Here's another drum backbeat. Again, the hi-hat provides steady eighths and the snare accents are on beats 2 and 4, but this one has some syncopation (see page 19) in the kick part.

Here is a perfectly workable bass part that doesn't do much for the rhythm.

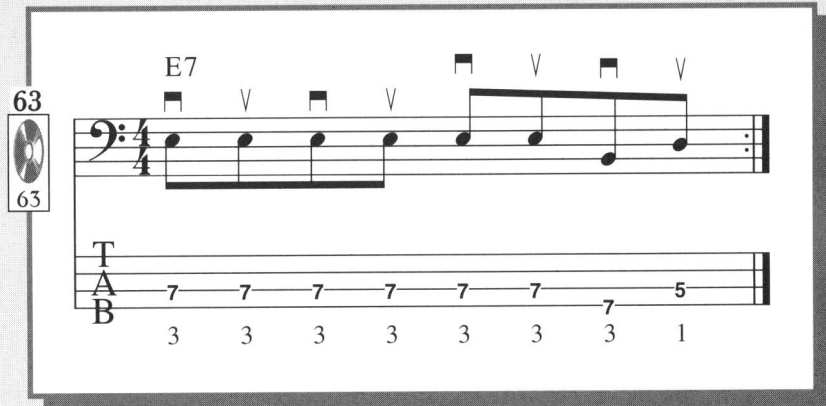

This one puts the groove right in the pocket.

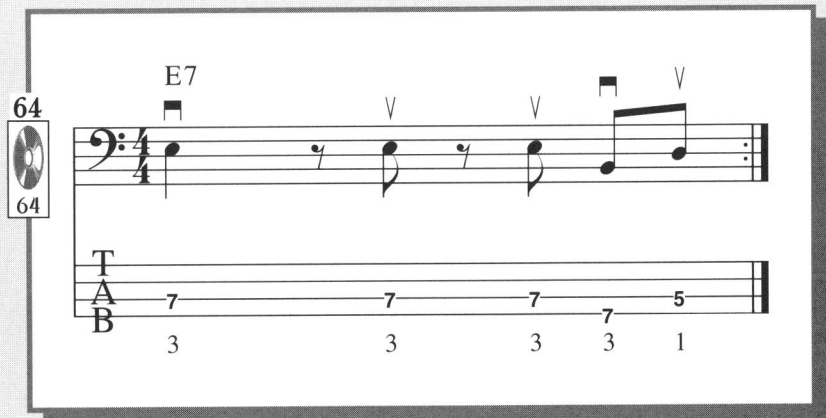

Here's another funky drumbeat. In this one, the bass-drum part is a little busier.

This line will fit over the drums, and sounds perfectly good, but does not really support the groove.

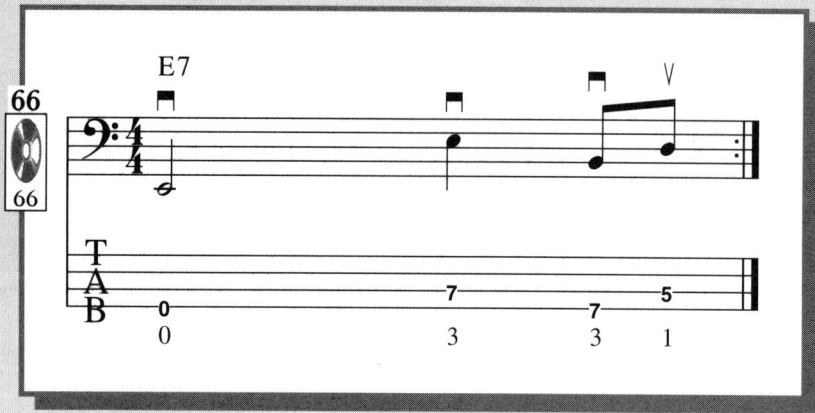

This line locks-in perfectly.

LESSON 23
Summary of What to Play, Lead Sheets and More

You never know what song or kind of music you may be asked to provide a bass line for on any given day. So far in this book, a number of resources from which you can choose to create these bass lines have been discussed. Here is a quick list:

- Arpeggios: the notes of the chord being played
- Major triad, pages 10–11
- Minor triad, page 15
- Diminished triad, page 20
- Augmented triad, page 21
- Dominant 7th chords, page 33
- The Major Scale, page 12
- The Mixolydian mode, page 32

Make sure that you have worked on each of the arpeggios in this list from numerous roots. In other words, it's great to know the patterns for playing a C7 arpeggio, but you need to be able to play them from any root, or you'll have to wait for a C7 chord to come along before you can play! Make sure you can do it on D♭7, D7, E♭7, E7, and so on. Pick a few roots each day and play every arpeggio pattern you know: major, minor, diminished, etc. Do the same thing with the two scales you have learned in this book, also.

Remember, the bass is tuned just like the four lowest strings of your guitar. That means that every scale you know on the guitar can be played on the bass. Most guitarists know some lead guitar scale patterns: the minor pentatonic scale, the major pentatonic scale, and likely a long list of modes. All of that is grist for the mill, too. Just play the bottom four strings of the patterns. Again, it is important that you practice these scales starting on all 12 notes.

THE SAFETY NET: THE ROOT AND 5TH

Unless you are playing advanced jazz, most chords you'll have to play under will have a perfect 5th above the root; we just don't play that many diminished (♭5) or augmented (♯5) chords in rock and blues. This means that there are two notes which are almost always safe for any chord: the root and the 5th.

MEMORIZE THESE ROOT-5TH SHAPES.

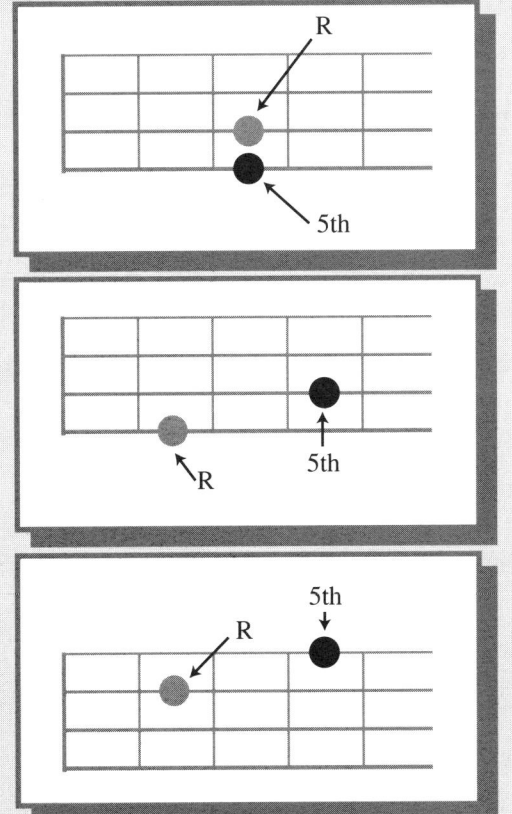

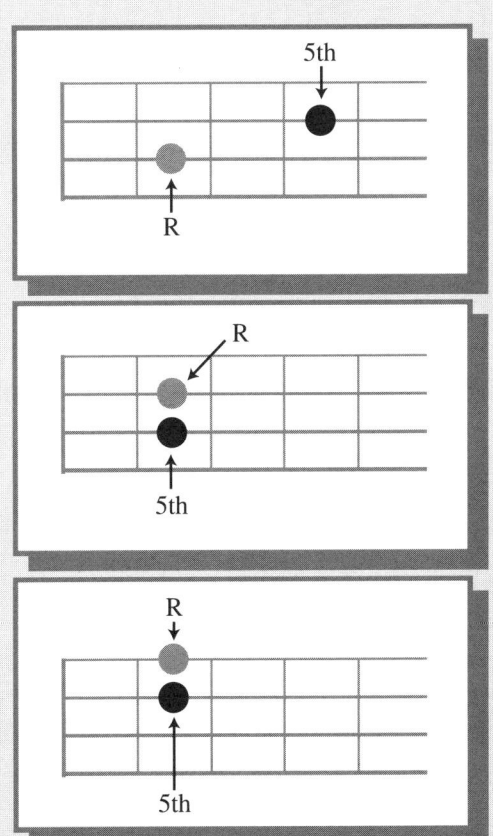

READING LEAD SHEETS

Armed with this ammunition, you can power yourself through almost any chord progression, whether you've had time to develop a bass line or not. Let's say you're handed a chart to play from which does not have a written bass line. All that's shown is the chord names, in other words, it is a common lead sheet. You aren't really familiar with the song, and may even have trouble if asked to strum through all of the chords.

△ = Maj7
-7 = min7

Whip out your trusty root-5th shapes and play without fear.

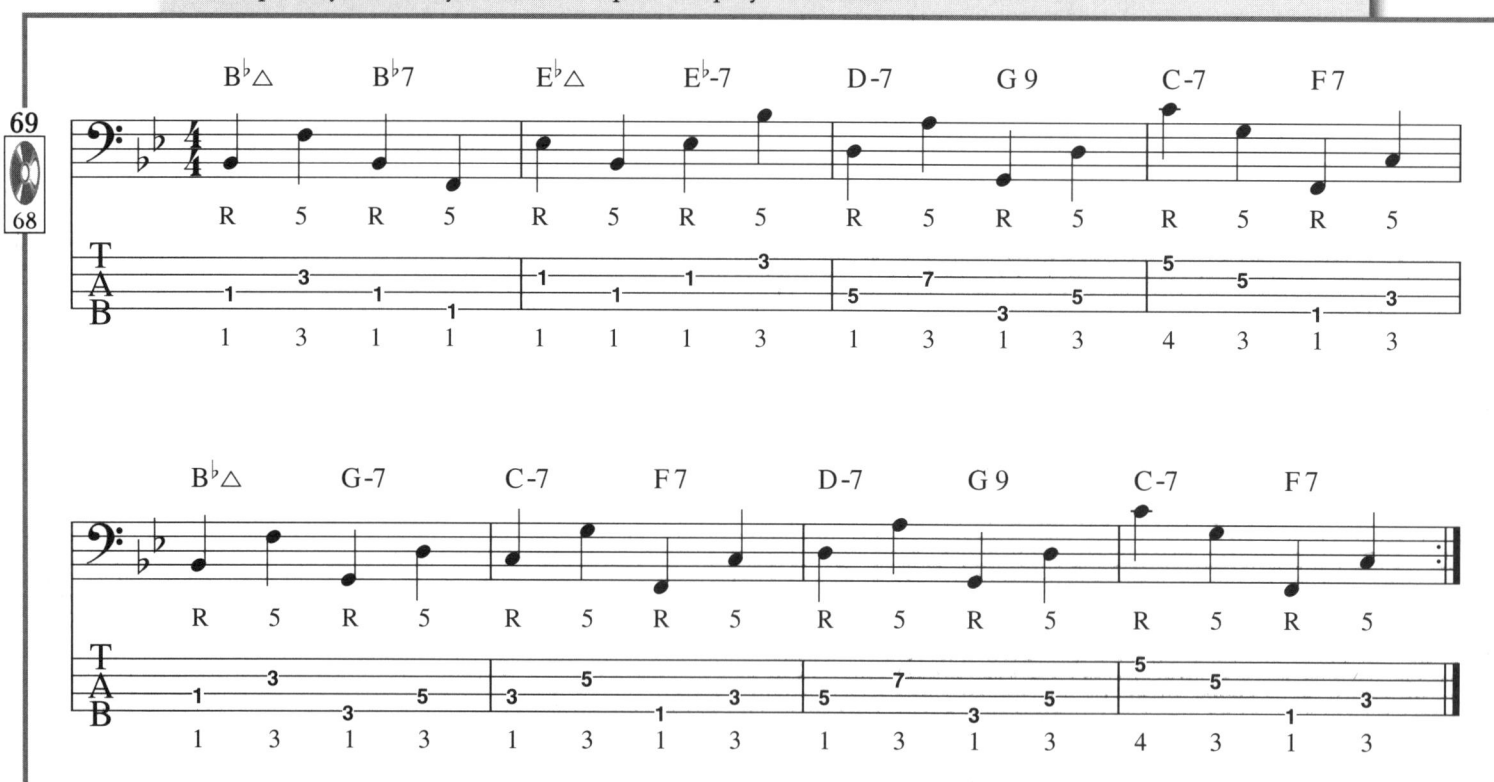

Listen to the drummer and do your best to lock-in. Your bandmates will think you're the best thing since sliced bread. After playing through the tune a few times, you'll be able to loosen-up and add in other notes from chords, impressing your fellow musicians even further.

Go to your local music store and buy one of the many lead-sheet style songbooks that are available. Some of them are called "fake" books, although nowadays, there is nothing "fake" about them. If they are out on the racks in the stores, they most likely comply with copyright laws and can be considered good sources for all of the "standard" tunes. You should stay away from illegitimate "fake" books sold "under the counter." They are probably not as reliable and are printed without permission of the songwriters or publishers.

Practice reading a few tunes every day, using every device you know for coming up with bass lines.

CONNECTING FROM CHORD TO CHORD

Once you have something to play for any chord, you will want to make the lines you play sound natural and smooth. Getting this kind of slick, thought-out sound doesn't really require a lot of planning ahead. You can get to the point where your playing comes naturally. All that you need is some stock tricks for getting from place to place, and a lot of general practice.

CHORD TONES THAT CONNECT

Often, one of the tones of a given chord will be a step away from the root of the next chord. Look for these and practice using them on the beat just before the chord change.

Sometimes, the 5th of a chord can be used as a connecting tone. Just make sure to move to the root that is closest.

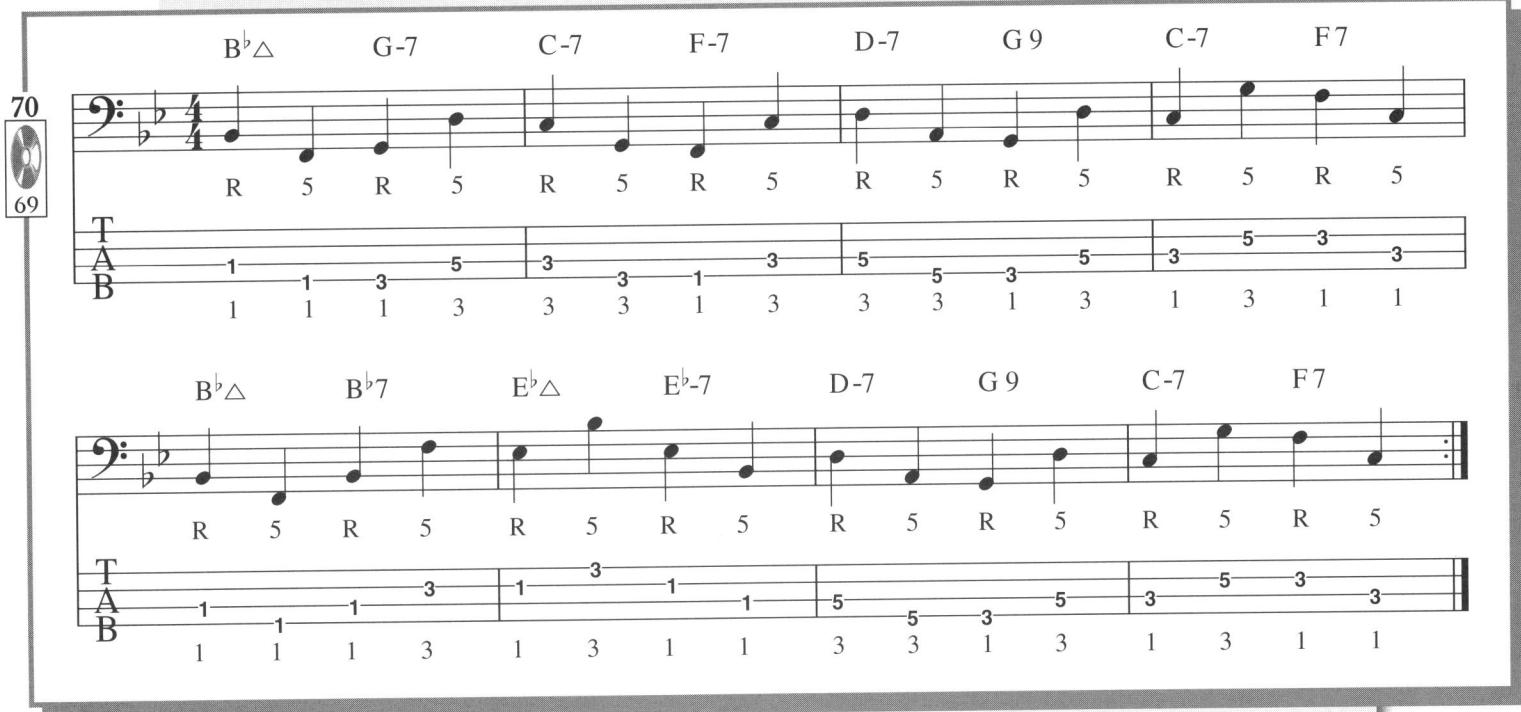

In this example, the 3rds of the chords can be used to connect to the roots of the next chords.

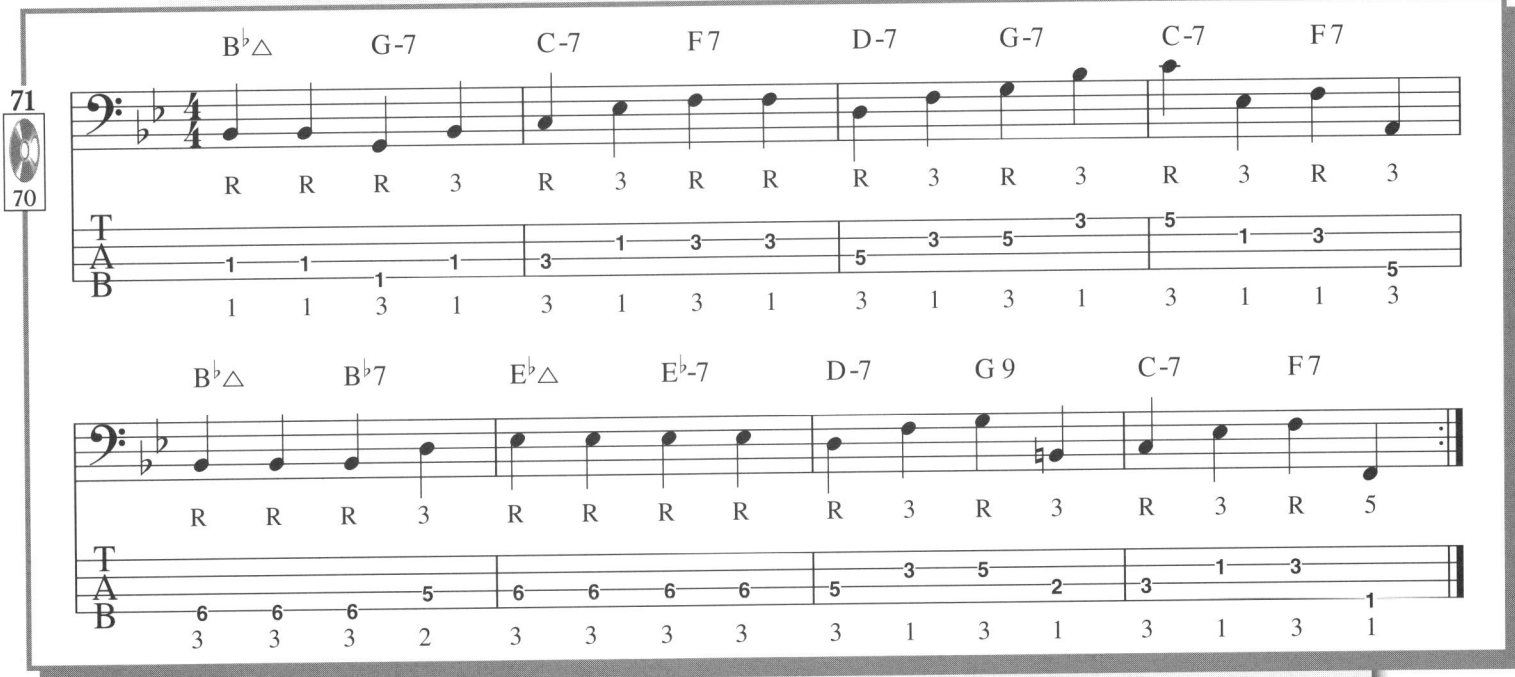

Experiment with using other chord tones (the 5th and the 7th) to connect from chord to chord, too.

In this example, both 3rds and 5ths are used as connecting tones.

STEPWISE LINES: WALKING

For the smoothest possible line, most of the movement will have to be stepwise as opposed to by 3rd or by 5th, as in the last few bass lines. This kind of line is often called a *walking* bass line. Another characteristic of a walking bass line is a steady, quarter note pulse with only occasional quick fill notes.

The best source for stepwise material is a scale. Let's look at how the C Major scale (page 12) can be used to create walking bass lines. Let's say the lead sheet looks like this:

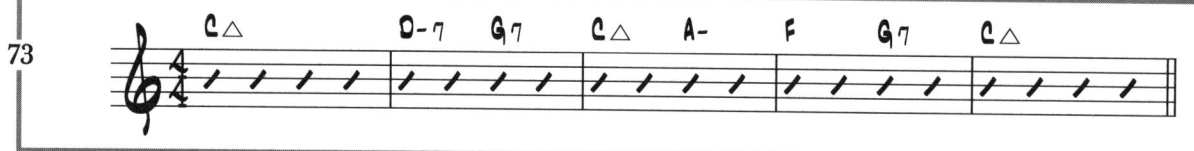

PASSING TONES

Using the C Major scale, we can create a bass line that will move mostly by step. The non-chord tones belong to the scale and are called *passing tones*. These tones smoothly connect one chord tone to the next. The result is a smooth, walking bass line. The passing tones are circled.

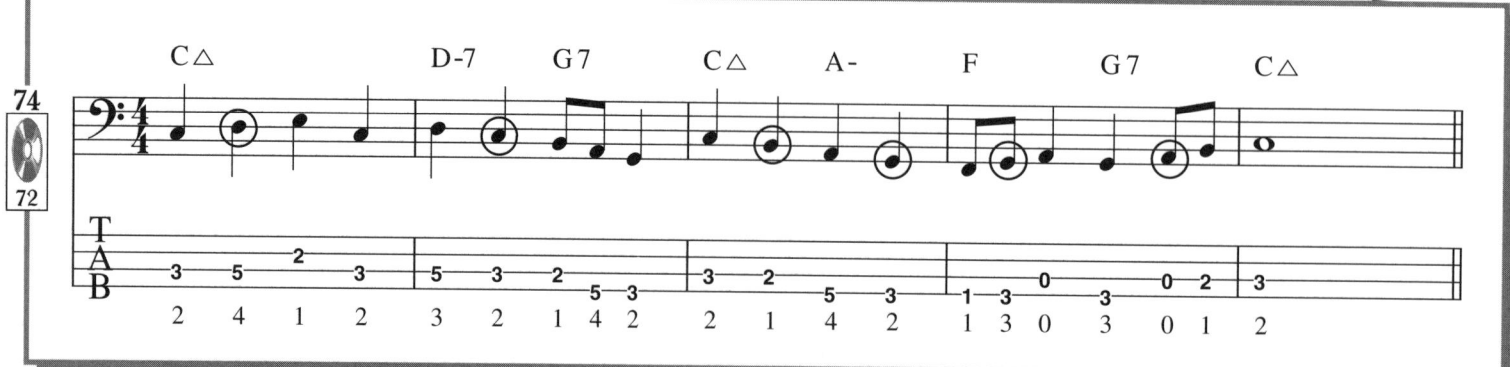

CHROMATIC PASSING TONES

Sometimes the passing tones we use to create smooth bass lines are not in the scale. Belonging to neither the scale or the chord, they are called *chromatic passing tones.* Here is another lead sheet.

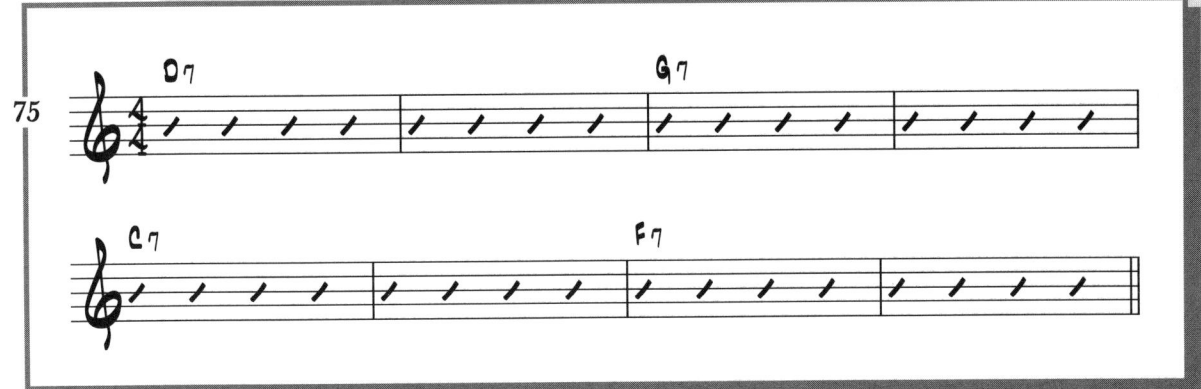

Notice that this bass line sometimes starts chords on the 5th rather than the root, which is always an option. Since the chords change slowly, think of using the major scale built on the root of the chord being played. The passing tones are circled. Chromatic passing tones are also labeled.

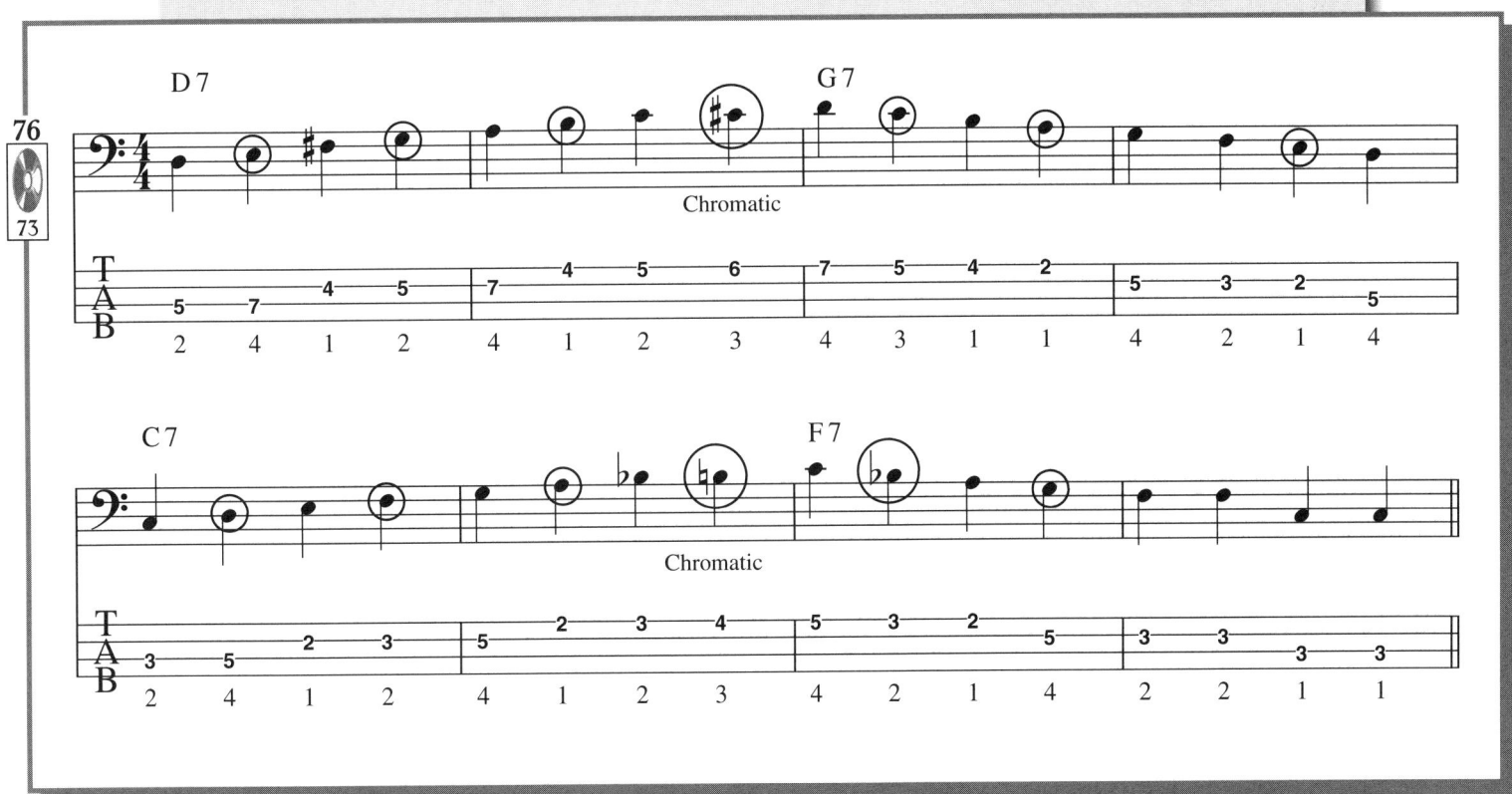

LESSON 24
Slap and Pop Technique

Slap and pop technique is one of the most important tools for the contemporary bass player. If your band plays any funk-based tunes, you will have to use this technique. Slap and pop technique actually combines of several different techniques into one distinctive style of playing. They are:

Hammer-ons (page 28)
Pull-offs (page 29)
Slaps
Pops
Dead notes

You already know about hammer-ons and pull-offs. Let's take a look at the other three techniques.

SLAP
Use the heel of the right hand to strike the string. Let the thumb bounce off of the string so that the strings is allowed to ring freely.

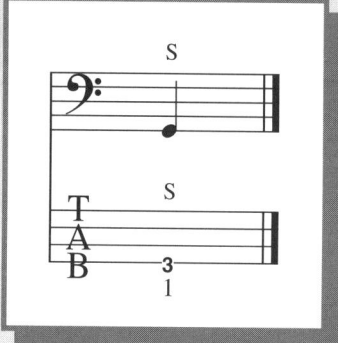

POP
Place the right-hand 1st finger slightly beneath the string (usually the 1st or 2nd string) and pull it away from the bass far enough so that it will snap back down forcefully against the frets to make a popping sound.

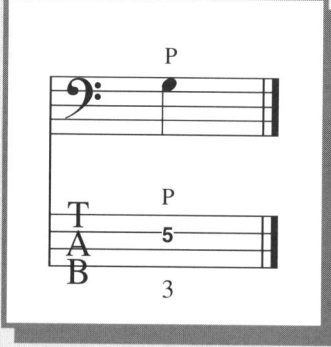

DEAD NOTE
A dead or muted note is produced by plucking the string while at least two left-hand fingers rest against the string, without pressing it to the fretboard. The sound is somewhat pitched, but mostly percussive. This is the same left-hand technique you learned for performing rests (page 18).

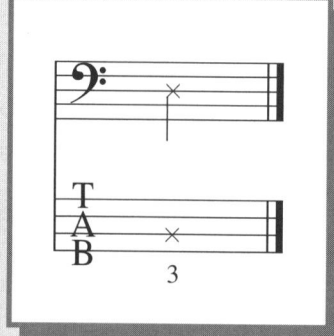
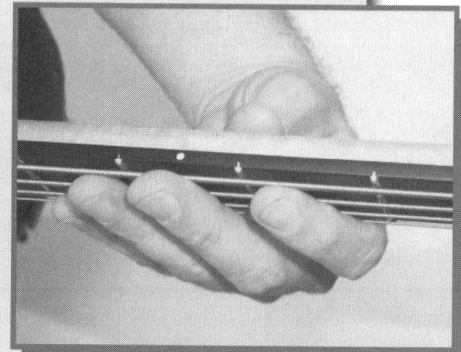

SLAP EXERCISES

Here are two easy exercises for practicing the slap.

Here are a few slapping licks. Notice that some of the notes are dead notes.

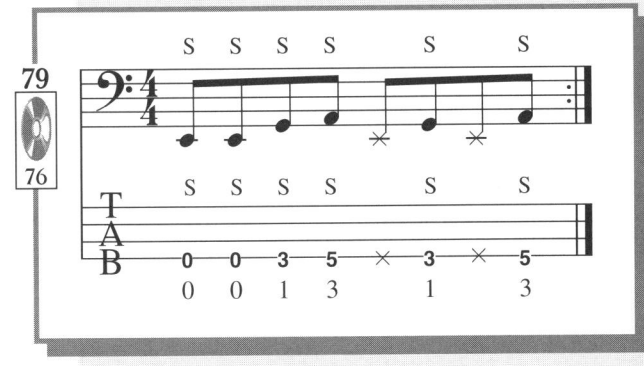

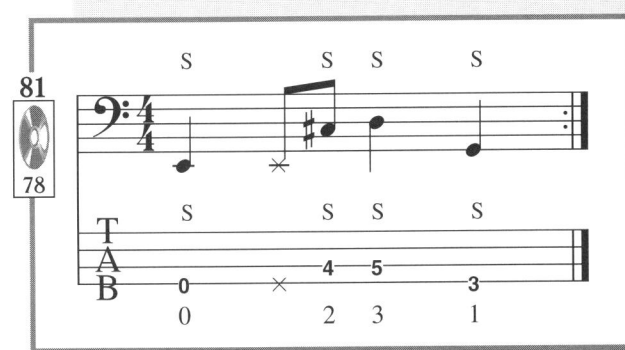

SLAP AND POP LINES

The pop technique is quite often combined with the octave shapes you learned on page 23.
Here are a few typical slap and pop bass lines.

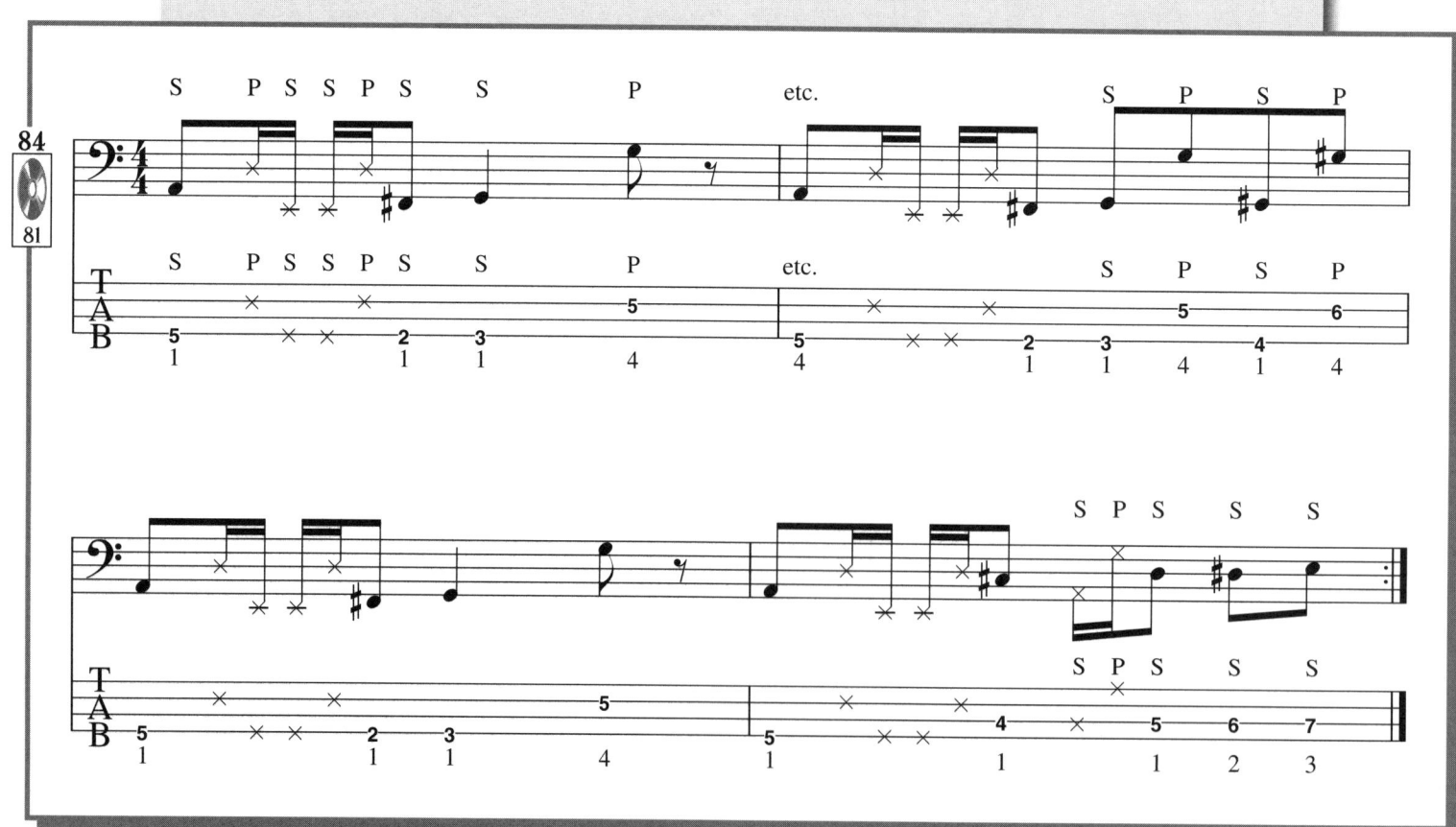

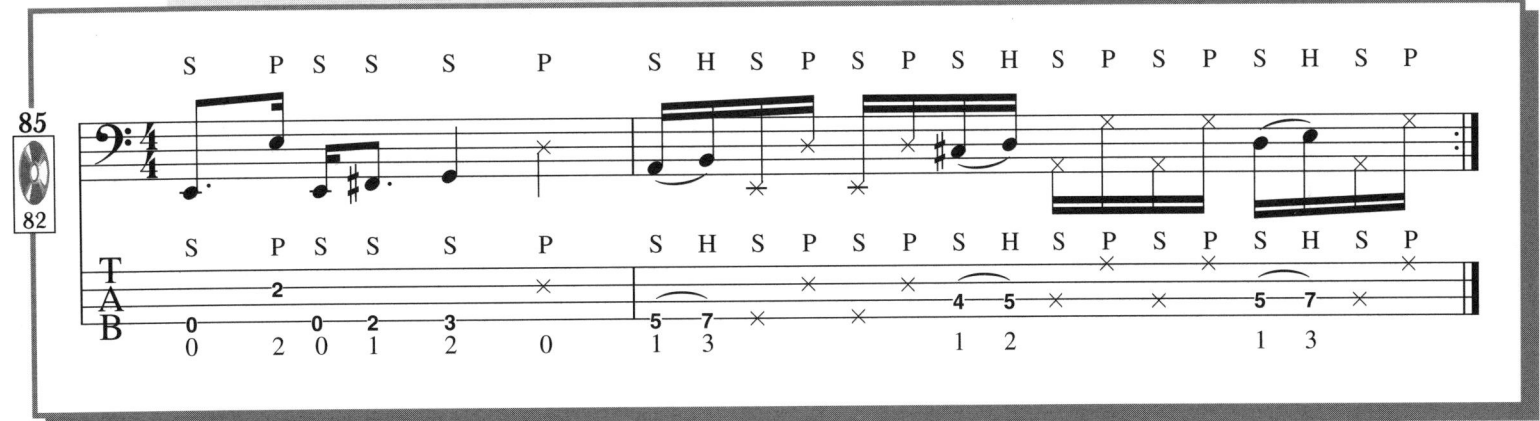

Congratulations! You have finished your introduction to playing the electric bass. You have accomplished a lot. You've learned arpeggio shapes to play under triads and 7th chords, tricks for playing lines under chords, a variety of techniques and articulations, developed your bass clef reading skills and become familiar with the fretboard from a bassist's perspective. You're ready for more! Check out *The Complete Electric Bass Method* by David Overthrow and keep working on your bass chops. Now, you should be an in-demand guitarist *and* bass player. Go get 'em!